MILLIONAIRE PROPERTY AUTHOR

How to Write and Publish a Bestselling Property Book

STEPHANIE J. HALE

www.CelebrityAuthorsSecrets.com

Copyright

Powerhouse Publications
94/124 London Road,
Oxford
OX3 9FN

Print Edition

British Library Cataloguing in Publication Data.
A catalogue record for this book is available from the British Library.
Cover design, editing, formatting by Oxford Literary Consultancy

For my children Cormac, Tierni and Chiara who shine light
on the world each and every day

Contents

STEPHANIE J. HALE

"The worst property books can be dull or 'samey'
... it's essential to have a powerful hook."

Stephanie J. Hale is a publishing expert who specialises in helping property investors to write, publish and sell their books.

She's spoken at property events around the UK including: The Ultimate Wealth Summit, The Property Super Summit and Progressive Property seminars.

She's founder of Oxford Literary Consultancy and author of award-winning books including, *How to Sell Over a Million Books.*

She's featured on BBC television, IRN, Radio 4, SKY Digital, and in national newspapers including *The Independent, The Telegraph, The Daily Express,* as well as numerous glossy magazines.

She's experienced in negotiating book serialisations and giveaways in partnership with international media.

The prospect of writing your own property book can seem daunting, especially if you've never written one before. How do you write a book that stands out from all the others? Do you have time to fit this into your already-busy life? How much value will it add to your business? These are all questions that you're bound to be asking.

In the pages that follow, you'll discover that many of the assumptions you have about becoming a bestselling author are wrong. It needn't take years, or even months, to write a book. It's possible to write your book in under a week if you apply and use the correct strategies. (Although if you want to include complicated spreadsheets or diagrams, it's likely to take a lot longer.) There is no need to hire an expensive ghostwriter. You can do this yourself, even if you're pressed for time or don't consider yourself to be a "writer".

Have you considered, for example, that by speaking your book into a Dictaphone, you can finish your manuscript three or four times faster than by simply typing it? You can then have this recording transcribed, edited and proofread ready for publication, within a matter of weeks. The key to success lies in planning your book *before* you get started so that that the quality is high from the outset and you are never left wondering what to write next.

I've brought together the leading property authors in the UK — many of whom I've worked with personally and professionally — to share their advice with you. They've been admirably frank about what it takes to turn a book into a bestseller. They debunk a lot of common myths, and some of their revelations may surprise you. You'll discover that becoming a bestselling author is perhaps more achievable than you once thought. As you read on, you'll learn step-by-step how to structure your book, and how to write it in a way that's appealing to your readers. I've also included a brief summary at the end of each chapter to give you an at-a-glance checklist of ideas that you can use for your own writing.

How do you sell a book?

I've worked with many authors, literary agents and publishers over the past twenty-five years. It still shocks me how little understanding most authors (and even some publishers) have about marketing. A lot of time is spent writing a book, so it seems crazy that many people trust in providence to sell it.

When you realize that readers take less than twelve seconds to decide whether to buy a book, and that seventy-four per cent of their decision is based on your book cover, it should help you decide where best to direct your energies. As readers are increasingly buying books online, you need a cover design that is eye-catching at *thumbnail size*. What looks fantastic at 6 x 9 inches, won't necessarily look good when it's only one inch high. You also need a memorable title and sub-title that shout, "Pick me up!" These days, your synopsis should ideally contain a lot of keywords that readers look for on search engines so that your book can easily be found on e-stores such as Amazon.

This guide will give you clear advice to help you choose a bestselling title, sub-title and cover. It also offers tips to help you write in an engaging way so that you hold your reader's attention until the final page.

How do you get published?

You may be wondering whether self-publishing or traditional publishing is best, or thinking about whether you need a literary agent. Traditional publishing, with its lengthy timelines, isn't for everyone. You may be impatient at the thought of waiting twelve months before you see your book in print and dislike the restrictions of the standard publishing contract. Terms and conditions in the small print, such as advertising competitors' books in the back of yours, or being prevented from creating spin-off products, rarely go down well with entrepreneurs. Alternatively, you may feel that mainstream publishing is a privilege worth waiting for and enjoy the kudos it brings.

Self-publishing, on the other hand, can be a sharp learning curve. You have complete control over the design of your book, and have the freedom to create spin-off products. You can also get your book published and on sale within days, or even hours. But should you have a bulk print run or use print-on-demand or opt for digital publishing? What price and discount should you set for your paperback, hardback and e-book? And where do you get hold of an ISBN barcode? The choices can be bewildering if you are self-publishing for the first time.

This guide will therefore help you decide which option is best for you so that you can produce a book to be proud of. There's no point investing time and energy in becoming an author unless it gives you a reason to hold your head high. By the time you finish reading, you'll be much clearer about how to pitch to a mainstream publisher or a literary agent, and what your choices are for self-publishing. You'll learn what works best and what doesn't, so that you avoid the traps that many authors (both new and experienced) unknowingly fall into.

Should you write an autobiography or a "how to" book?

All authors are different. Some feel comfortable writing about their professional experiences and personal life. Others prefer to write a handbook filled with facts, information and statistics. You can write a serious and weighty tome. Or you can have a pocketbook with lots of humorous cartoons and graphics to get your message across. You can also have a combination of these things. There is no clear right or wrong!

What matters most is how much *value* you are giving to your readers. But to do this, you have to have a clear idea of *who* exactly your audience is from the very start. Are your readers beginners to property, intermediate investors with a small portfolio, or seasoned experts? Are they looking for detailed information, or something inspirational they can dip in and out of? This knowledge will influence the type of language you use and the contents that you include. It should also help you decide which vector image or picture to put on the front cover. If you're brave enough, you may also include a photo of yourself!

Writing about people you know and things that have really happened can be very powerful in a property book. If you add dialogue, this is like a bolt of electricity that brings events to life off the page. The reader thinks, "Oh my God, this really happened. These are real people. Wow!" They *experience* your book at a deeper emotional level, rather than simply *reading* words on a page. It's the difference between feeling like you're being taught, and being actively and enthusiastically engaged.

How do you write a book that readers want to buy?

A common concern is whether your idea is too similar to another author's book. Yes, the worst property books can be dull or "samey." They can be overloaded with technical information and mathematical calculations guaranteed to send readers into an instant snooze. This is why it's essential to have a compelling hook or a powerful story. You want to be remembered for entertaining and educating, rather than curing insomnia!

For this reason, I recommend that you spend time doing market research on Amazon to see what other bestselling property authors have written about. Just because a book has already been published on your topic doesn't mean it's already been "done." If you look at the readers' reviews, you'll soon find out what they loved and what they felt was missing. You need to write the book your *readers* want, rather than the book *you* think they need.

I recommend that you make a detailed checklist before you start writing. Ask yourself questions such as:

- What is it that my readers hope for and dream of?
- What are their problems and challenges?
- What are their anxieties and fears?
- How can my book help them?
- What proofs can I offer of my credibility and expertise?
- What is the trigger that will make them seek out my topic?
- Why would they not buy my book?
- Why will they choose my book rather than a similar one?

What about marketing and promotion?

A common misconception is that mainstream publishers will do your book promotion for you. These days, authors are expected to do the lion's share of publicity and marketing for a book, both online and offline. This guide will give you lots of ideas for tastefully launching and promoting your book — even if you feel that it's outside your comfort zone.

You'll learn about various aspects of promotion such as:

- Launching a bestseller campaign.
- Getting your book into stores like WH Smith.
- Organising a successful launch party.
- The best ways to get reader reviews on Amazon.
- Attracting media coverage in national newspapers and glossy magazines.
- Creating a buzz on Facebook and other social media.

Are you ready to get started?

Think of all the leading property gurus, and most of them have written a bestselling book. A book can transform you from expert to "authority," and from unknown to "celebrity." It can be the launch pad that catapults you into the limelight and makes you stand out from your competitors. It is a powerful business card, which is why so many property experts and trainers give away their books for free or offer bundles of their books when they speak at conferences. No doubt you've read one or two of these books in your time!

If you're like most property experts that I work with, you've probably spent a lot of time educating yourself and attending seminars. You'll be experienced in finding trustworthy tenants and flexible mortgage brokers. You'll also know about deals that go wrong and business partners who let you down. Your life will have been filled with achievements to be proud of, as well as challenges you've learned from. If so, the first draft of your book is already written. You just have to coax it out of your head and onto the page.

If you'd like advice on whether your book idea is marketable, please do feel free to contact me at: **oxfordwriters@me.com** and I'll be happy to help. I wish you massive success with writing and publishing your book. I know you'll be celebrating your achievement for many years to come!

IDEAS FOR YOU

- It's possible to write a book in under a week. If you include spreadsheets or diagrams, it will take a lot longer.

- Seventy-four per cent of a reader's buying decision is based on your book cover.

- Your cover must be eye-catching at *thumbnail size* since most books are bought online.

- Your title and subtitle must be attention-grabbing. They should ideally contain keywords in order to be optimized for search engines online.

- Traditional publishing may mean waiting twelve months to see your book in print, and a restrictive publishing contract. However, it brings kudos.

- Self-publishing gives you control over the look and feel of your book. You also have freedom to create spin-off products. However, it can be a sharp learning curve.

- You still have to do the lion's share of promotion even if you secure a book deal with a mainstream publisher.

- Before writing your book, consider if your readers are beginners, intermediate investors, or experienced experts. Adjust your language and contents accordingly.

- Treat your book like a product you are launching into the market – do some research *before* deciding on your topic.

- Make a checklist what your readers want from a book and what will make them buy yours.

- Look at other property books on Amazon. Readers' reviews will tell you what they are looking for in a book.

- Plan your book structure *before* you start writing. This will keep you in the flow and help you avoid writer's block.

- If you record your book on a Dictaphone, it will be finished much faster than if you type it.

- Libel, confidentiality and privacy laws should be taken into account if you write about real people.

- Use dialogue if you can, as it brings people and events to life.

ROB MOORE

"I can get a book done now in a week, or maybe eight days."

Rob Moore is a self-made businessman, sought-after speaker and author of four bestselling property books.

In 2005, he was struggling to make ends meet as an artist, selling his work for less than it was worth, and building up a debt of over £30,000.

He's now a multi-millionaire property investor and co-founder of Progressive Property, and has bought and sold over 350 properties since 2006.

He's appeared on prime-time TV shows for Channel 4, the BBC and The Business Channel as well as featuring in the *Financial Times* and *The Wall Street Journal.*

He's shared the stage with the likes of Sir Alan Sugar, Bob Geldof, Karen Brady and James Caan, and holds

the Guinness World Record for the longest speech in aid of charity.

His taste in shirts and his shoes upset stuffy businessmen. He especially likes helping young entrepreneurs, and [extra]ordinary people who don't have silver spoons or inheritance.

I've written five books: four with my name on, and one together with my business partner, Mark Homer. That one, I wrote with him in The Bahamas. The first version of the first book, *The 44 Most Closely Guarded Property Secrets* was written at the end of 2007. We launched it privately — it wasn't on Amazon — and we were selling around four hundred a month just privately through our website.

Then we launched it on Amazon, and it became a bestseller in all property and business categories. Then the crash kicked in, so we wrote a book called *Make Cash in a Property Market Crash.* That started to outsell *The 44 Property Secrets* — perhaps an extra one hundred copies a month.

We used to do events around the country — we still do — and we used to sell our books at events. That's how we sold four to five hundred a month privately. Then when we launched it on Amazon, it became a bestseller in the property and business categories. You already know the launch model. We do a one-day launch where we get partners involved, and we offer a one-day deal where if you buy a book on the day, you get a discount and a couple of bonuses. That model bounced us right up to the top of the bestsellers' list in the categories that the books were put in. What we'd find with that is the book would go right to the top of the two categories and would stay up there for three or four days. Then it would kind of settle back in the top twenty.

Then, we did a book that was basically a load of successful case studies from our students called *Progressive in Property: From Beginners to Winners*. When we published that, we were a little more market savvy. When we launched that, it went to No. 5 in every book on Amazon. So literally, if you went onto Amazon it was: *Fifty Shades of Grey 1* was top; *Fifty Shades of Grey 2* was second; *Fifty Shades of Grey 3* was third; *Fifty Shades of Grey trilogy* book was fourth; and then *Progressive in Property: From Beginners to Winners* was number five. So a little property niche book got to No. 5 in every single book on Amazon on launch.

You can imagine at our office (we have thirty-five people who work for us), we were all jumping up and down all over the place like *The Wolf of Wall Street* movie. We never expected that at all. We knew we could get to the top of the categories, but never in our wildest dreams did we think we'd get to the fifth bestselling book on Amazon. I believe there are a hundred million Amazon users, and we thought, 'Wow! This is unbelievable! How did we do that?'

We just got more partners involved. We did a book launch where if you bought a book right then, you'd get a discount, but you'd also get a couple of tickets to an event. That stayed as No. 5 on Amazon for a few days, as normally people buy a few days after.

Then we just followed that launch model with my book *Multiple Streams of Property Income,* which got to No. 4 of all books. Then we followed it with my partner, Mark Homer's book *Low Cost, High Life* which got to No. 3. So that's three of my books that have been in the Top 5 of all books in the UK and the other two in the property category.

Excellent. You wrote one of the books with Mark and in The Bahamas. Explain how it works writing with somebody else.

Obviously you're a book coach Stephanie, and you know that unless people fully immerse themselves often they just never finish the book. I'm a bit different because I can sift through it in my head using a stream of consciousness, so writing a book for me isn't difficult. It's the editing process that I personally find difficult because once I've done it, I don't want to tweak it fifty-eight times.

So when I first started, I'd literally just get up at 6 a.m., get a really strong coffee and just try and do it until 6 p.m. or 7 p.m. with a couple of breaks. I knocked out the first two books in about three weeks doing it like that. I didn't have as much knowledge back then, but my business partner did. So I'd literally write a bit and think, 'I need more content.' Then I would interview Mark, take notes, and I'd go back and fill it in. So I was writing, but I was interviewing Mark a lot, as he had all the information in his head, but he didn't know how to write a book.

Each time I've written a book, I've refined the process. I can get a book done now in a week, or maybe eight days. The best thing to do is to completely isolate yourself and ensure that there are no interruptions in your life or your world. I've found that the best way to do that is to get abroad. Also, if you've got a goal to write a book in nine days, and you're on Sandy Lane in Barbados, as we were for one of our books, and you're spending £20,000 on an amazing hotel, and you're flying first class, you're not going to mess around and come back with fourteen pages. Mind you, that's a justifiable business expense because you're going out there to write a book! So each time we've gone abroad, we've gone somewhere nicer, somewhere high class because it forces you to write that book. You've almost got no choice but to finish it — so now I can write a book in about eight days.

I knew I was never going to be able to get Mark to finish his book because of distractions and the difficulty for him of getting it out of his head. So I bribed him, if you like, with this trip to Sandy Lane. I just got him up at 6 a.m., stuck a coffee in front of his nose, and we just sat in coffee shops overlooking the beach. I had the laptop, and I just got him to start sharing. I was writing and taking notes, and every time something good came out, I would push him for more detail. So I was basically writing it and taping it, but I was also stoking his fire of creativity to get all of the gold out of his head.

I've actually got the sixth and seventh book we will be doing. We've got nine days booked in Dubai, at a five-star hotel and I'll do the same there. I seem to have a model that works, and we'll probably have our sixth and seventh book by mid next year.

Many people might ask why you would write another book when you're already so successful and have so much else going on in your life? What drives you?

Why set another goal? Why grow your business every year? If you've got a good physique, why carry on going to the gym? For me, life is about challenges. One of my biggest values is continual improvement, and I realise that when I achieve something or when I grow, develop or learn. The journey is never done. So I can imagine I'll write forty, maybe fifty, books in my life. I don't know for sure, but there's always something new to help someone with;

there's always something new to teach someone. Also, I just feel each time, I can do it better. I'm going to do an updated 'version 2' of one of our books at the end of the year. Someone said, "Why do you need to update it?" My answer is, "Just because I love it, and I want to get better every day every year." I'm still in my early thirties — if thirty-five counts as early thirties! I want to be doing this when I'm eighty-five or ninety. I just have a desire to grow and learn, to have fun, to enjoy the journey, and help others.

The anxiety many new authorpreneurs have is that if you write a book, you're giving away your best material for free. What's your opinion on that?

I have a very clear belief on that: I believe you should give away your best stuff. If you give your crap stuff, or if you hold a lot of it back, people will think you don't share. I learned this a few years ago. One of our property businesses probably does about £5 million a year, and that's all on courses and training. I literally dumped everything I knew from this into my first book. And yes, people would have said the same thing to me, "Why would you share it all in a book?" Some people say, "If you do share it all in a book, they won't want to do your courses." But there's books, then there's attending live events, then there's being mentored, and then there's partnering with people. I remember someone saying to me once, "Course training is dead because with the Internet you can learn everything online, etc." It turns out that we grew our business while that guy is now working in a pub! Events will never be dead. Events, live courses, training, mentorship, will only be dead when people don't want to be with people. If it were enough to just read a book and then say, "I'm a millionaire now," everyone would do it! So you can read a book and get the information, but then you need help, support, accountability, mentorship, love, connection and the feeling of being around people.

So I think that if you write a book with a load of amazing information and don't hold anything back, then people will think, 'Wow! If I can learn that in a book, what could I learn with them at an event or being mentored by them?' So I'm a big believer in giving away as much as you can because you earn people's respect by doing that. The point is that you want to educate people.

You have a great photo of Bob Geldof holding your book on your website. Tell me about some of the other things you've done to promote your books, as well as the giveaways and free bonuses.

We had to encourage him to do that! He was a lot of fun Bob was. I guess we do as much as we can. You will also see pictures of people like Lord Sugar and James Caan holding the book or reading the book, and I think that probably helps. I wouldn't say that it sells millions of them, but it certainly doesn't do any harm.

Brian Tracy [business guru and bestselling author of *Eat That Frog*] read one of my books and sent a really glowing testimonial, which was really great. Those kind of celebrity endorsements really help. Having it on Amazon and learning how Amazon works, certainly helps. It was something I didn't understand a few years ago, but I think each year we're getting better at it.

We'll soon be changing the name for the first book because we know the keywords everyone searches for on Amazon. You know about my recent posts on Facebook, and the smart thing is to find out what everyone is searching for on Amazon, and then call your book that instead of calling it what you want to call it. So that definitely helps, as being seen on Amazon is quite a massive thing. We do a lot of speaking events promoting the book and have a 'bundle' deal to encourage people to buy several books at a time.

You've had appearances on Channel 4 and BBC television, as well as being in *The Wall Street Journal* and *The Financial Times*. Is media publicity a big part of your marketing?

I remember we had just written the first book, the *Property Secrets* book, and *The Independent* phoned us up and there was a two-page spread on buy-to-let. It was in and around the crash period, and that was right off the first book. So that was quite a big win: a double-page spread in *The Independent* when you're only one year into your business, based on your book.

Two full-colour pages is worth about £30,000 worth of advertising.

If I'd known that, I'd have asked for four pages! Mark and I were quite young in business, and young guys. We had a photo-shoot outside some of our properties, and they wrote an in-depth article. We've still got that on the wall in our office. So that was directly off the first book, and yes definitely it gets you speaking opportunities, and it gets a lot of people to our events.

We've done a book called *Multiple Streams of Property Income,* and we have an event by the same name. So a lot of people will buy the book, and then they will come to our event. The event will probably produce £2,000 per head revenue, in terms of what it's worth to our business. So a book is a good lead generator for our events. If you partner a book with an event, that can make it quite special. We've had a lot of media appearances and we often get offers. We've done at least five or six pilot TV shows that didn't air, as well as the ones that did. Often journalists just Google us, and if your books are high up in Amazon and appear on Google, then that works really well.

There are a lot of property books out there — how do you separate yourself from all the other property authors?

Well, our company name is Progressive, and our company values are progressive. I remember when I first got into property, and I was learning from all the gurus out there. You could put them in a box of how they looked and how they talked and how they acted. They were all wearing grey suits and white shirts and all very officious. It wasn't "me." I'm kind of a disruptive, vocal, passionate, somewhat Tourettes type of an individual, and I just thought, 'We need to shake this industry up.' I don't think people want to go to these "stand behind a lectern, very dry and official" talks. I think people want motivation and inspiration. They want someone they can relate to, who's had struggle and hardship and isn't stand-offish. So we slapped on our bright shirts and went out on some sort of mission. I think it's very clear if you look at our industry that we are just completely different from everyone else by a long shot. We own a space of being innovative, disruptive, and always adapting to a changing market, which is really important in property because it's continually changing. If you don't change or jump on change, you get left behind.

We are now the biggest training company in the UK for property. We did that within six years. Sometimes our industry is a bit guru-filled, and people look up to these gurus who own loads of property. The gurus get a wee bit too full of themselves, and I probably got sucked into that a bit. Once I had bought twenty or fifty houses, I really felt "I am destined to achieve something in my life, and I can stand on a stage and share that."

Some people see you as a guru. But I learned maybe five years ago, it's not the guru that people want. They are inspired by the guru, and the guru can lead. But what they want is a community of like-minded people where they feel part of it, where they don't get put down, or they don't have negative people. So we have built a huge community. There are loads of people doing JVs [joint ventures] and working together.

Mark and I have pretty much stepped back from it now. We probably run two hundred and seventy-three training courses a year, and I used to do every single one. Now I only do about a quarter of them. We have great trainers who believe in the brand and the vision and a bit of a movement, if you like. That's how I'd say we're unique.

It's all very well being good at what you do — but if nobody knows about you, then it doesn't matter how brilliant you are. Do you think that having bestselling books, and embracing PR and marketing, give you extra leverage and get you in the public eye?

Totally. I was quite lucky because I did some courses on marketing in the early days of our property training business. I learnt then that the only way you are an expert is if you are *perceived* as an expert, and you are seen in the world to be an expert. Our industry is a good example of this. If you look on telly, you look at a lot of the famous people who do property on TV shows, and some of them, they don't have many properties. I've met a lot of them. Some of them don't have that many 'buy to let' and some of them don't have any at all. Mark and I have nearly four hundred now. In the first year, we had fifteen properties, two years in we had forty-five properties — more 'buy-to-let' than many of these so-called TV experts on ITV and Channel 4. But they *were* TV presenters, and they *were* very good at presenting on television. They had a *brand*, and the world knew about them. So that's what makes an expert — the perception of it. So over the years, Mark and I have tried to bridge the gap where we are genuinely good at what we do. We genuinely have a few hundred 'buy to let' and we do walk the walk. But at the same time, the world has to *know* that we are walking the walk — because if they don't, we won't have a business. There are so many people in the world who are great musicians or great painters or whatever, but they never get seen and therefore they don't exist. I guess you could say that Progressive is as much as a marketing business and a brand, as it is a property business.

You have over sixty reviews on *Multiple Streams of Property Income* on Amazon. Explain whether you did anything to solicit these reviews or if these were all organic.

If you look at *44 Secrets*, we have about one hundred and twenty reviews; on *Multiple Streams*, I think we have sixty; on *Make Cash in a Crash* probably sixty; on Mark's book *Low Cost, High Life* about thirty. They are all different. The *Multiple Streams of Property Income* we launched on one day. What I did was I got everybody in my office to read the book, and then to comment on the book before the launch. I felt it was genuine as I asked them to read the book; it's not like they put dummy reviews on there as I know that does go on. But at the same time, it's twenty per cent cheeky as I had twenty-odd people in my office. They all read the book, and they all put a comment on, and because I had twenty comments, that was a good start.

But it does cause a bit of an issue actually because if you look at the reviews there are about six poor reviews. Basically, some people who bought the book on the day were like, "Twenty reviews on the day of the launch; they've got to be dummy reviews," which they kind of weren't. But I suppose you could say twenty per cent were solicited. So the first twenty reviews to get the critical mass were from people I knew. I would definitely recommend that to anyone writing a book, get twenty copies, give it to your friends and family, and get them to read it to get some reviews.

With Mark's book, we didn't do that because we didn't want that same thing again. So those thirty reviews are all organic. With *44 Secrets* and *Make Cash in a Crash* the reviews are all organic. But what we do to bump them up now and again is, in our community, we say, "Hey, have you read any of our books? Go and put a review on Amazon if you liked it, and we'll give you a free book of your choice." So there's a couple of ways we've done it: we've launched and given it a push, or we've let it be organic and then when we think it needs a few more, we ask our community. Obviously they have to have read it, as I just don't believe in doing dummy reviews.

I say, "Write whatever you think; you can be honest," as I think if you've got fifty or so five-star reviews it looks a little bit fake. I give them a free book — so you can tantalise someone to go and put reviews on, but I think you have to be ethical about it.

A lot of authors are nervous about getting negative feedback from readers. How do you feel about negative reviews on Amazon?

Traditionally, I'm a soft, warm, cuddly, meek, mild, don't-want-to-upset-anybody kind of person. So that scared me putting myself out there in case someone had something negative to say. But I think I've got over that now. I think I'm quite well-known in my industry for running my mouth off; in fact, I've got a World Record for it [Laughs]. I just think it's fine. If you look at Lord Sugar, there's probably five million people in the UK who have something negative to say about him, and they haven't even met him. They watch a TV show and think they know him. So I think if you don't have anyone saying anything negative about you, then you're not big enough and you're not getting your word out there enough. Every human being is different; we all have different values. Therefore, someone is always going to have something negative to say about you if you do what you do, because they will by nature be the opposite of you. So I find that a bit of an honour and a privilege now if people do that. I think if I've got a hundred reviews naturally, I'd expect to have at least five reviews that would be no good. That's only natural.

No book is going to have a hundred five-star reviews, so let them bring it on. In the old, old days I used to really want to go and defend myself. It felt unjust and unfair. Nearly every review that we've ever had about us on forums have been from people who have never met us or don't know us, but they make it up that they have. But normally, our community will go and defend us. So bring it on!

E-books or physical books — which have been doing better for you?

Physical. I think e-books have little to no value any more. I can imagine people have downloaded twenty or thirty e-books and never read them. In the world of online, where everything has an 'e' in front of it, I think something that's physical has more tangible value. Don't get me wrong: as a

29

lead magnet as we call it, e-books work. But I would say e-books get read less than physical books from what I know, and they are just not "sticky". If you pay £12-£15 for a book, you're probably quite likely to read it. It's physical and you can touch it. So I prefer books definitely.

Over the years at events, I've sold books in bundles. So I'll sell five books in a bundle and give a free gift away with it. How many people e-mail me saying, "Rob, I read this e-book you wrote. It changed my life"? A handful! How many people say, "Rob, I read your physical book and it changed my life"? Thousands. So that's the proof.

Some property books are priced at £29.99 and others are as low as £5.99. How was *your* pricing decided on?

I'll be honest: I'm still struggling with this one. I'd love your advice at some point, as I'm not sure. When we first launched, we said, "You know what, we're going to go for £15 plus. Hey, this is property, this information is worth a lot of money." So, a) we wanted to give that perception of "it's worth something," and, b) we expected that if people paid £15 instead of £5, they'd be more likely to read it. We felt they might be a bit more "sticky" as a customer — because the more you pay for something, the more you value it. I think it depends on your strategy. We've done a lot of research, and if you look at the Amazon books that seem to organically sell the most, they seem to be the ones at £4.99, £5.99 or £6.99. So when we've launched our latest books, we've launched them at £9.99 or £8.99 and it seems that we've sold a few more.

So I think it depends on your strategy. I think if you're privately selling them and you do events and you're a speaker, I think you should whack a good premium on. No one who has met you for an hour is ever not going to pay

£15 or £20 for a book. Then you sign it, and it adds a little more worth and they value it. The jury is still out on this; I'm still kind of learning. But if you want to go and whack your book to the top of Amazon, I think you probably want to be £5.99 to £9.99.

If I pay £25 for a book or one for free, I know which one I'm reading first. But at the same time, the sales will be of low volume. So when people search for your book on Amazon, I know the amount of sales and the conversion of sales has a big impact. But I'm still learning on this.

Yes, that's spot on. You can whack the price of a book up to £24.99, and it puts a higher premium on the information. If someone is really committed, price is irrelevant. But it's a different strategy ... Mainstream or self-publishing?

Well, we've always done self-publishing and never done mainstream. So quite frankly, I've had no experience of having a publisher and maybe in the future we would. The reason we didn't go down that road is because I just wanted my book out there. I'm the kind of person where I've got an idea and I want it done this morning. I think, 'If we have to go down the road of involving a publisher, it could take a year, it could take two years. So that was the first reason: I just wanted to get it out there.

Another thing is that I didn't want to be restricted on how I sell my own books. Also, at the time when I wrote the first book, the property market was just dying out in a big way. Property became very unpopular with the masses from 2007 to 2010. Whereas we were getting approached all the time by the media pre-2007, it was suddenly like property didn't exist. So I didn't have any confidence that a publisher would want to publish a property book at that time, but I still wanted to write books.

I'm at a point now where I'm writing books numbers six and seven, and I'll probably write number eight at the end of next year. I'd probably be open to looking at that if I felt a publisher could fulfil our needs, or they could give us more reach. But I have spoken to some publishers, and they really don't give any marketing guarantees. So why else would I want them to publish it? I think, 'So you're not going to guarantee any reach for me, so what's the point?'

In the past, it was because traditional publishers had global distribution and got you into bookstores. But, of course, many books are bought online these days, not in bookstores. So that model worked ten years ago, but maybe not today.

Sure, and we've still managed to get one of our books in Waterstones and WH Smith. We just phoned them up and they said, "Yes, we'll stick a couple in, and if it sells we'll stick another couple more in." So we stick a couple in, and then my mum goes out and buys them, and then they stick a couple more in. It's funny. My mum, who works for us, managed to get us in a few local bookstores. I do know authors who have had a traditional publisher, and they pay a big lump sum like £15,000 or whatever, and they'll get them in WH Smith in airports and stuff like that. They will put a stand out for you if you pay enough, and you can go take a photo of it. I've not got a lot of experience in how that works. I would probably be OK to look into that for a new book.

Yes, that's true some authors pay for the privilege. There are two main contacts in North America for getting books into airport stores. Talking of new books, do you still feel excited when a book is launched?

Yes, when we launch it our whole office is on it all day. We're constantly refreshing the stats to see how far it's gone up the rankings; what number it is; if it goes up into the Top fifty, Top twenty, Top fifteen. It moves up fast, then starts to slow towards the end of the day. We then update Facebook or Twitter, or send a few e-mails out to try and get it up higher and higher. It's a massive buzz. I don't get nervous as I know how it works now, and I know we're going to get into the Top Five. We've got enough partners and that kind of thing. But I get really excited, and I love the buzz.

IDEAS FOR YOU

- If you have a business partner, interview them for content for your book to get the "gold" out of their head.

- Don't be afraid to give away your best information. It will inspire people to come along to your events and be mentored by you.

- Get celebrity endorsements if you can, as these help boost sales.

- Find out what readers are searching for on Amazon, then call your book this instead of calling it what you want to call it.

- For an Amazon bestseller campaign, offer a one-day deal with a discount and bonuses if readers buy your book on the day.

- Partner your book with an event — for example, giving both the same name. A book can be a great lead generator for events.

- Perception is everything. It's not enough to be good at what you do. You need to be *perceived* by the world as being good at it.

- Encourage your staff, clients, family and social media followers to read your book and put reviews on Amazon.

- Expect around five bad reviews for every hundred reviews on Amazon.

- E-books have lower perceived value and readers are less likely to read them.

- Consider your strategy when pricing your book. A premium book price (e.g. £15 to £25) gives the perception that information is "worth something."

- A low book price is better for high volume sales. (Amazon books that organically sell the most seem to be priced around £4.99 to £6.99.)

- Sign the front of your books — it adds to their perceived value.

- Phone up Waterstones and WH Smith to ask if they'll stock your book. Ask friends and family to order it in the store for you.

- Be innovative. If everyone else is wearing grey suits and being officious, don't be afraid to wear bright shirts and be disruptive!

STEVE BOLTON

"We give away around two thousand to three thousand books a year."

Zero qualifications, five companies, more than two hundred franchise partners, £200 million+ of property purchased, four kids, one thousand+ talks, three books, two boats, twenty-six fishing rods, one R8 and one painful business failure!

Steve is bestselling author of *Successful Property Investing* and co-author of *The 7 Biggest Mistakes Made by Property Investors.*

He's founder and chairman of Platinum Property Partners (PPP), which is the world's first property investment franchise, and is also the fastest growing premium franchise in UK history.

Steve has featured in TV shows including *Property Pensions, Head to Head* and *Property Kings* on Sky Overseas Property Channel, as well as Channel 4's

Dispatches documentary, 'The British Property Boom'. One of his mentees was also featured on Channel 4's *Secret Millionaire*.

My parents were not particularly rich, so my enduring memory of my childhood when it came to wanting things was: "You can't have that, we can't afford it" or "You're going to have to save up." At such an early age, I became frustrated with not getting a new bike or a computer, or things that I wanted, and so I became driven to find ways of making money.

I was lucky in that both my mum and dad were inspirational. My dad used to work down the pits in Lancashire but was born with a talent for football, which he developed. He eventually became a professional footballer, but back then, this didn't make my parents the Posh and Becks of Bournemouth — we were still a normal working class family.

My mum came from a pretty poor background. She trained as a hairdresser, then when my dad retired from football in the 1970s, he bought a high street shop for about £4,000. It was a burnt-out shell, and he worked really hard to turn it into something he could be proud of. He converted the upstairs into a two-bedroom flat and downstairs into a hairdressing salon, which my mum ran as a business. I used to help him with the refurbishment at the evenings and weekends.

After living in the flat above the shop for about six months, my dad bought a huge property which comprised sixteen flats. We lived in one and rented the rest of the units to tenants. In the summer, my parents used to rent them as holiday flats, and I would go in with my mum, sister and dad, and we would clean them and meet the tenants.

So, I got my first taste of property investment, development and running a business when I was very young and unknowingly, I grew up with two entrepreneur property investors, albeit on a small scale. I laugh to myself when I think about the fact that I grew up in an HMO-type property and now have been responsible for the acquisition of a portfolio worth more than £200 million!

It was my parents' drive and hard-working nature that encouraged me to look at ways I could earn money. I never had a silver spoon in my mouth and was always taught to be independent and self-reliant. And as I got older, I realised that having money wasn't just about having material things, but more about having financial security for your family, freedom, and the ability to give back.

Did you go straight into property from school?

No. My first proper job was teaching kids outdoor pursuits. I soon realised that teaching, coaching, training, mentoring and seeing people develop is something I was very passionate about. I was good at it, and I found it highly rewarding. From then on, I knew I always wanted to be in the people development business — and every business that I've had since has had that as a core principle.

I started to read a range of personal and professional development books that inspired me to go it alone. I became tired of working for someone else. I was working full-time – seventy to eighty hours a week — at an outdoor pursuit centre as a manager and instructor. I was in my early twenties, but I was only earning a very low wage, and I realized that I wanted to be in control of my own future.

I wrote to a guy who built an outdoor adventure trail, and I basically said, "I'll do the marketing if you build them." Within three years, we were the European market leaders. Everything was going great. At the beginning of 2002, I was riding a wave on paper. I was a millionaire, with a great level of income, and a six-bedroom house overlooking the sea in Dorset. Then suddenly, it all came crashing down around me shortly after the terror attacks of September 11th 2001, and the foot and mouth outbreak.

I found myself in a three-bedroom rented bungalow with a leaky roof, and my wife was seven months pregnant. My son was born into uncertain surroundings in this dilapidated bungalow, without me really knowing what the future would hold.

And that's how your property journey began ...

I called it the 'best worst experience of my life.' On the one hand, it was devastating, but, on the other hand, I had a clean start. I realized that the fact that my previous business premises were rented meant that I didn't have the protection of underlying or appreciating assets. At the same time, it was my house that had saved me from bankruptcy — we sold it and released the equity. So I went back to my roots and started to think about property as my parents had done.

They say ninety per cent of the world's wealth is made or held in property. Andrew Carnegie, the richest guy who ever lived, was credited with that quote. And my dad was living proof that it could work on a small scale. That's when I started reading books, getting educated and finding mentors. I was fortunate enough to have been in business, so I had good connections. In the meantime, there was a product that I imported from America, which I bought for

$7,000, and I had a small team of people who would sell it for £15,000. We only needed to sell two or three products a month, which is what we did. I outsourced everything and had no staff, so very quickly I had £100,000 annual income from this little business, which I could use to start building a property portfolio.

In America, I came across the concept of rooming houses, which is basically where blue-collared workers would live together in duplexes, quadplexes, apartment buildings. So I was thinking of investing in America, and then I realized that was crazy: I had a family and a wife. I wanted to find something I could do in England. So, after two years of very expensive research, I had viewed hundreds of properties, I had been on scores of training courses, and I had read every single property book that was available. I had done a huge amount of learning and research and knew that my next business needed to be built on the basis of high income and capital growth.

I was very risk averse because I had been wiped out by events outside my control. So I was constantly asking myself, 'What can go wrong?' and 'How can you address those things if anything does go wrong?' I concluded that if I had a very high income-producing buy-to-let property portfolio, then that would be the key to creating financial security for me and my family. So that's when I came up with this investment strategy. That was is 2004. Ten years on, and I've set up a business that has helped more than two hundred people achieve the same or are on a tried, tested and proven path to doing so.

A big part of your own journey involved reading books and getting educated. Is this why you felt compelled to write your own books?

I am a firm believer in continuous learning, which is why reading so many books formed part of my research — I still read books on a weekly basis now. I learnt so much and was grateful that these people were willing to share their expertise with me. When I reached a point where I felt I had knowledge and information that would be of value to others, I wanted to share it.

Another motivation for writing a book was a marketing masterclass that I attended with Jay Abraham, who is a billionaire marketing guru. I always remember him saying, "A book is the best business card you will ever own."

So, a book is not only a way of giving back, but purely from a business perspective, it gives you credibility. It acted as a marketing funnel for us. The statistics are that for every one hundred people who buy one of my books, one of those will end up becoming a Platinum Partner. It gives them the opportunity to get an insight into the model in their own time, and at the very least they learn something from it.

One of your books was co-authored. Describe how the process worked for you when you were authoring a book with someone else.

Co-authoring a book can take many forms. For me, it was very simple.

I had been giving a talk on the *7 Biggest Mistakes Made by Property Investors* for about two years. There was a detailed table of contents and the structure and a lot of information in the presentation. I worked with one of our marketing and PR team to get the contents transcribed and down on paper. I then worked on these transcripts when time would allow and started putting the book together. If there were gaps or important details missing, then we would have a meeting to talk about how we could add value. These meetings were transcribed and that content would be added to the book.

At the time, I was also launching the franchise. Someone who worked for me was interested in becoming one of my business partners, and so I offered him co-authorship of the book. We prepared a biography for him, and he wrote an additional chapter, with a bit more about his background and his story. So he co-authored a book that he needed to provide very little input for — that's basically how it worked.

Tell me about your process for writing the second book, *Successful Property Investing*. What lessons did you learn from the first?

About three years after writing *The 7 Biggest Mistakes*, my business partner and I went our separate ways — we both had different goals and motivations. This was the main catalyst for writing *Successful Property Investing*. If you have both books, you'll know that eighty per cent of the content from the first book is in the second book, but my business had moved on and there were things I had learned along the way that I wanted to include.

Over the years, I had thoughts and ideas or remembered a story that I thought could be added to the book. I just wrote a brief e-mail to myself and kept all those e-mails in one folder. I then worked on the revision and editing myself when I was on holiday.

A great book I'm reading at the moment is called *Seven Basic Plots*. It states that there are really only seven plot structures for any story, any book, any movie that has ever been written. It is just a variation of these seven plots, and some of these stories have three or four of these plots in them. That's what I've found in business and in life generally — there is always a way of creating a system to accelerate you towards your goals.

One of the things that's striking about your books is that you share the secrets of your success, but you also share your mistakes. A lot of people would veer away from doing this. Did you feel exposed by doing it?

I think that comes down to your personal values. I value openness, honesty and transparency. Many times, people have come up to me after a talk where I've shared how I was wiped out and had to start again. They couldn't believe I spoke about my experience and found it so refreshing. In America, failure is just expected. They say the average millionaire loses their fortune three times before they finally learn how to keep hold of it. Certainly, I've done a range of investments over the years. You know that four out of ten businesses you invest in are going to fail; two or three might give you your money back; one or two might double or triple your money, and hopefully, on one, you're going to get ten times the increase. If you're in business for any period of time, you are going to have a business failure. I think sharing that in an honest way is a good thing to do. Everybody loves "the hero's journey" — we like to see someone who was down and out, succeed. Certainly in the British culture, I think you get respect for it. It also demonstrates that you are open, honest, and you have integrity because you're telling the truth.

One of the key points in your books is *"why you should run a mile from anybody who mentions no-money-down property investment."* That's likely to make you unpopular with some gurus in the property world! Do

you think that writing a book is about putting your head above the parapet and saying things that other people don't dare to?

I have a lot of respect for people who tell the truth, whether it's popular or unpopular. You can't have respect without walking the talk and doing it yourself. So, for me, I find life in many ways to be very simple. If you just tell the truth, it makes life very straightforward. So I couldn't with congruence and integrity say that no-money-down is really good and really easy.

Is it possible for someone to buy a property with none of their own money? Of course it is. If your mum, your dad, your aunt or your uncle lends you the money, or they go on the mortgage with you, or supply the deposit and other costs as a gift or a loan, it's completely legal — that can be done. Can you do a joint venture with an investor, where you bring the deal and all of the work and the time, and they bring the money and it's fully legal? Yes, you can do that.

It's not that no-money-down deals don't work. What I object to is the way it is promoted to just put bums on seats in seminars. The message attracts people with little money and very little experience. They are sold this kind of pipe dream, "You too can be a property millionaire and start with no money and make an absolute fortune." I just think it's wrong: it's factually incorrect and misleading. You look on a lot of the websites and think, "My God, everybody is successful that does this." There's a guy called Dolf de Roos who did what I understand to be the most comprehensive study of real estate training courses over a twenty-five-year period. His conclusion was that only three per cent of people who attended property courses had actually gone on to buy an investment property. In other words, ninety-seven per cent of people were failing. So to say with no-money-down, you can make a fortune is wrong. That's my fundamental issue. I think people should tell the truth. People may not like it, but at least you will be respected for it. At least you can debate and argue, and stick up for your point of view because it's what you truly believe.

What do you actively do to promote your books day to day?

As a company, we use my book as a marketing tool, another touch-point for prospects. As soon as it was published, my main channel for promoting the book was at the end of a talk that I (or somebody else from PPP) would give. We'd also make sure that effective SEO and Amazon listings would make sure the book could be found. But we didn't have an external promotion strategy and go on radio shows or TV programmes to promote the book.

We give away around two to three thousand books a year. People read the book, and then when I meet them at an event, they are already familiar with me and our business. It's just a case of putting a face to a name. It's a way of building and nurturing relationships.

In the early days, it was a fledgling business, and I had built a decent-size portfolio but nothing record-breaking. Yet, because I had written a book and we had a DVD as well, people would read the book and watch the DVD. Then when they met you, they'd think, "Oh my God!" because they'd seen you on the TV screen, so it was almost like meeting a celebrity. That's how we used it.

A lot of authors would be horrified at the thought of giving away three thousand of their books each year. I

understand why you're doing it, but explain this strategy for someone else who doesn't. What's the impact on your business?

From a purely business point of view, we know what the lifetime value of a Platinum Partner is to the organisation — not just financially but just as importantly, what they can add in terms of experience, knowledge and support to others. The books are one of those touch points that helps somebody to make the decision to join PPP. I know we've got a lot more Partners because of the book because it generates the interest in the first instance. It's a no-brainer that we get the book out there.

It's "freemium" content that we are giving away to help educate and to give back some value and knowledge, but it is also a tool for use within the business.

You get a lot of media coverage and have been featured on several TV programmes. Has this just organically evolved?

Getting media coverage is about having something interesting to say that people want to hear. However, it's not an easy thing to achieve, and for a PR campaign to be a success, you must be proactive and surround yourself with good people from a good agency. They are the professionals, and they have the contacts.

I'm a great believer that if it takes one hundred thousand words to write a successful book, it's going to take you four hundred thousand words to launch a successful PR campaign — you need to put around four times as much effort into the PR and marketing to really make the book (or whatever you're trying to sell off the back of the book) a success. We've got a very newsworthy and interesting business, and we work with a PR agency. That's why we're getting the majority of the coverage that we're getting today.

You have some great book reviews on Amazon — particularly notable is that of Simon Woodroffe, the founder of YO! Sushi. He says, "I trust this guy. Read this book, do it now." Did you feel hesitant about asking high-profile people to review your book — because many first-time authors are initially?

It's about building relationships, and I'm always conscious of this when I meet people. I met Simon through a not-for-profit, Peace One Day, that I dedicated the book to, and we got to know each other. One day, we got together, and I told him that I'd already written a book. I asked if I could give it to him and would he mind giving me a quote. So he read the book in about a week and then sent me the quote.

Interestingly, I get asked for quotes for other people's books all the time now. I've got a shelf in my office for books where I've quoted on them or where I'm quoted in them. Authors love to quote on other people's books because if you have an interest in the subject matter and you're quoted in the book, readers are more likely to look you up and buy one of *your* books. So it's a self-perpetuating cycle where authors are endorsing each other.

One of your specialties is to combine the mercenary — i.e. making profits — with the missionary and giving back. That's an important part of what you do isn't it?

My philosophy is to: Be More, Do More, Have More and Give More. I think everybody should go through life with a kind of visual metaphor in mind. They should be having one hand up — reaching up to people above them that have achieved more than they have, with a view of getting a lift up to the next level. At the same time, I think everybody should also (no matter what level they are at) be reaching a hand down to help other people. It would be great if everybody went through life paying it forward.

Quite often, people miss out on giving. To give effectively, you also need to be able to receive. Like you said, some authors feel uncomfortable asking other people for endorsements and quotes. That to me is a practical example of an underlying challenge with asking and receiving, and being the recipient of somebody's goodwill. I think most human beings want help and need help. People tend to be good at giving or good at receiving, but I think you have to have a nice balance of those two things. So at a philosophical and practical and personal level, it's about having one hand up and having one hand down and thinking every day, 'How can I help others?' and 'Who is helping me?'

There is an old study, that's quite often quoted, which basically says you should look at the five people you spend the most time with: friends, family or business associates. You should then average out how much they earn, their level of health and their level of happiness. If you average that out, that is one of the best predictors of how your life is going to turn out. I am a great believer in that.

Mark Victor Hanson says, "Your network equals your net worth." Therefore, to have mentors, friends, business partners and associates who have actually achieved more than you, is one of the things that makes the biggest difference. When you spend time with millionaires and billionaires, you learn from these people. You learn how they treat other people, how they manage their time, etc., and you can pick up on the things that you want to replicate. There are some really striking differences between what high-achievers do.

So giving back gives you a good feeling inside. You're helping other people, but you have to be willing to receive support and ask for it, as well.

IDEAS FOR YOU

- If you have a business, use your book as part of your marketing to generate leads, customers and clients.

- Use your business talks and presentations as the content for your book. Record this information, then get it transcribed and edited.

- Write emails to yourself with your thoughts, ideas and stories for your book. Keep all these emails in one folder so you can add them to your book.

- Everyone loves "the hero's journey." Be honest about your mistakes and challenges.

- Voice opinions and beliefs even if they're unpopular. You'll be respected for it.

- Consider giving away your books to prospective clients and partners. This is an excellent way to familiarise them with you and your business.

- Writing a book and being an author can give you celebrity status with strangers when you meet them for the first time.

- Put four times more effort into your PR and marketing than you do into writing your book.

- Consider working with a professional or a PR agency for a successful promotional campaign.

- Give away "freemium" content to help educate new clients and give value to them.

- Don't be afraid to ask for testimonials. Authors love to quote on other people's books, especially if they have an interest in the subject matter.

- Dedicate your book to a worthy cause or charity. Be a giver as well as a receiver.

JIM HALIBURTON

"The more information I put out there, the more people seem to come on my courses."

HMO Daddy, Jim Haliburton, is a star of the BBC show 'Meet The Landlords,' author of over ten books and manuals including *How to Become a Multi-Millionaire HMO Landlord* and regularly writes articles for property magazines.

He began investing in property in 1991, letting rooms to students while he was a college law lecturer.

By 2004, he decided to leave his job and buy investment properties full-time. He now owns a letting office as well as over one hundred HMOs, thirty single lets and has twenty-four rent-to-rents.

He is also in regular demand as a speaker at property meetings around the UK, runs courses and mentorships on the business of being an HMO landlord. He is unique

in the business in that he lets people work in his property business to learn the skills of being an HMO landlord and gives tours of his properties.

The reason I decide to write books is complex. I'm not sure about the motivation — I think it's therapy! I find that if I write my thoughts down, it helps. The first book I wrote, *How to Become a Multi-Millionaire HMO Landlord*, was really for my children to show them how the business works, so it's an explanation for them. As a college lecturer, I used to do a lot of writing, producing hand-outs for students, it was a form of creativity. As for writing now, it's changing. Now I suppose I'm looking to write to improve the HMO Daddy brand. It's to promote my HMO courses and because no one else is doing it. One of the good ways, I am told, to get yourself known as an expert in your field is by writing books. And it's just taken off — I've got so much written. Above all, I love writing.

It's the finishing that I find the most difficult. I've written ten books. Starting to write a book is very simple and easy, it's the re-writing, the re-drafting and the changing that I find takes most of the time. If I could get rid of that, I'd probably get books produced very much faster.

Tell me about your writing and editing process.

I wrote my first book back in 2005 — that was eventually titled *How to Become a Multi-Millionaire HMO Landlord.* I never really finished it because after writing and rewriting it, I'd got so sick of it, to the point that I couldn't stand it any more. It only takes seven hours to read, but I have rewritten and amended it so many times I have had enough of it!

54

The way I do it is to write by hand and then I give it to my secretary to type. She usually misreads what I've written, so I have to correct that, and I think of something else to add, and so it gets read and read and read. I've probably read my own book more often than all the people who have bought my book and read it!

After writing my first book, I started to write stuff to update my book and to give more detail because I was so averse to going back and re-reading the first book that I'd written! For example, *Planning and HMOs* — this originally started off as an alteration to a chapter, but then it grew into a separate book. With my first book *How to Become a Multi-Millionaire HMO Landlord*, I needed to change the bit on planning. Then, I ended up making planning a separate book because I had over the years learnt so much more about the subject that it justified a book by itself.

Can you still remember all the titles of your books?

Well let's try: *How to Become a Multi-Millionaire HMO Landlord*, that was the first one — you always remember the first one. The second was *Operating Standards*. That's how to operate an HMO business, it gives the procedures for operating the business. The third was *Forms, Agreements and Letters for HMO Landlords*. The object of the second and third books was to make running an HMO a 'turn-key business'. The fourth one was *DIY Eviction*. I'm struggling now ... I'll just try to remember them, probably not in order. *HMOs and Compensation for Unlawful Eviction ... HMO Daddy Reveals All ... HMO Landlord Rules and Joint Ventures*.

How about the latest one: is this one book or two? It started off as *20 Money-Making or Saving Tips for HMO Landlords* and the next revised edition will be *35 Money-*

Making or Saving Tips for HMO Landlords. Have you lost the will to live yet? [Laughs]

There's another book. It's in the process of being written now. *A Tale of Unlawful Eviction or Extortion* – it is sitting in a corner. That's more a novel about my experiences of being sued – thankfully unsuccessfully – by an ex-tenant who alleged he had been unlawfully evicted. I suspect it was not the first time the tenant had tried suing his landlord.

Why did you decide to write a novel aside from your non-fiction books?

I was sued for unlawful eviction. So it's based on real events, but fictionalised to avoid a libel action, so names have been changed. It's so daft that I do not think people will believe it to be true. As they say: fact is stranger than fiction, and in this case it was.

I was mortified over being sued. It's a crazy system. I had to write it down to appreciate how crazy it was myself. If you could put yourself into a position where you end up being faced with the best part of £100,000 worth of damages and costs. It was therapy for me to write about it.

The obvious question is: you're incredibly busy, and yet you're also prolific in writing books. Why do you keep writing them?

I don't think I am prolific. This is the subject if anything you could say, of laziness. I've been writing the same book since 2003. These other books are all spin-offs of the first book. *Operating Standards* is a spin-off from *How to Become a Multi-Millionaire HMO Landlord* – it became a separate product as the book had grown so large.

Originally, they were together. I wrote my first book for my children so they would know how to run the business if I wasn't around; the second book was to show them and my staff what to do. If you can do it for one business, you can do it for another HMO business; it's the same thing. That manual could be used by other landlords. That's why it became a product that I can sell.

HMO Forms, Agreements and Letters is another manual plus CD or USB. I've reproduced the forms, agreements and letters I use in my business. Again that was done for myself, but I decided to monetise it. I just took all the forms I use, depersonalised them, and offered them to other landlords. Why reinvent the wheel? I've found that eighty per cent of your business letters are the same thirty letters. So if you write a letter, keep it and once you have written about thirty you will build up a file of eighty per cent of the letters you will ever write. Then all you have to do is change the name and address and a couple of the details, and you've written eighty per cent of your letters. So you keep something like thirty letters that get repeated all the time. The result is you only have to write them once or with HMO landlords who buy the manual and CD copy and adapt mine.

HMO Daddy is an integral part of your marketing and branding. How did this name come about?

Well, I used to go and talk on Ranjan Bhattacharya's courses. Ranjan is another landlord guru who occasionally runs courses — he is very good, well worth listening to. One of his crew, a bubbly bloke said: "I've got this lovely title for you: HMO Daddy," and I thought, 'Well, I have to have a name. I may as well call myself HMO Daddy.' The HMO Expert was another one I considered using.

But HMO Daddy sounded good until I got someone who I employed to market me, and he said: "I can't market you Jim ..." after he had agreed to it and we had spent ages discussing it, "... because I've just discovered that HMO Daddy also means homo-daddy!" It is a term used by homosexuals to describe someone who pays for sex with young men. I was amazed I had not realized this, but by this time I had been using it for a few years so I decided to stick with it. This may be why my website gets a lot of hits!

Well, it's certainly memorable! [Laughs] How long does it take you to write your books in real terms? Do you do a regular hour a day, or do you cut yourself off and write solidly for a week? What's the process?

Every book is different; there's no standard process. I had children late in life, and I don't know if you've read children's bedtime stories, but they are one of the most boring things on earth [Laughs]. So I'd be putting my son to bed and reading a bedtime story at seven o'clock. A big joke in my family was: "Daddy's asleep." I would fall asleep at seven or eight o'clock at night and wake up at three o'clock in the morning. What do you do at three o'clock in the morning? Your mind's going, your head's clear — and unlike my earlier life, you're not suffering from alcoholic oblivion or hangovers — so I just started writing. I would write for three hours at a time, and that is a lot of writing.

I'd write, then come into the office and give it to my secretary, and she would spend the rest of the day typing it up. She just couldn't understand where all this stuff was coming from; she thought I'd written it previously and could not grasp that I had written it that morning, and if she checked the ink it was still wet. The early hours are when I'm most prolific; the words just flow. Then it slows right down because it comes into the tedium of re-reading what you've done, amending it and refining it. Or someone points out something that you haven't explained very well, so you change that, and you think of something else or a better way of expressing a point. So I am forever re-writing.

The latest book I did was *20 Money-Making and Saving Tips for HMO Landlords*. When I started that, I did ten tips while I was running a course as 'filler' when people came back at the end of a break. I would say: "Right, what sort of tips can we have?" As there were a few other HMO landlords in the room, we were just throwing around ideas.

It was so simple; I just knocked that together. But then I went through it, revised it, changed it, and other ideas came to me for the rest of it — so it just carried on growing. On the last revision I did, which was two days ago when I was on my holiday, I got up to thirty-five tips. That's my problem: I can never finish a book. Every time I re-read it and correct it, I come up with something else to add to it or I think, 'That could be expressed better or expanded on.' It's a never-ending process.

So how do you reach your decisions on what to keep in your books and what to leave out?

I don't leave anything out; I tend to add to it! Every time round, the book becomes bigger and bigger. The only time I take anything out is if it's wrong or it's libellous. I've made a few quid flogging my books. I self-print them. My office staff staple them together or put them in a file. Most of them are written as manuals. *How to Become a Multi-Millionaire HMO Landlord* was originally written as a manual in a loose-leaf format. *DIY Eviction* and *Operating Standards* are also manuals.

With my first book, a few people came back and took the mickey out of me for a few spelling errors – like saying 'brought' instead of 'bought.' I hope most of these errors have now been corrected. I'm not very good at proofreading!

One of the things I hear property experts worry about when they're writing a book is that they may be making themselves redundant by giving away all their best information. For example, people may not come to your training courses or mentoring programmes once they've read the advice in your books. Is this your experience?

I quite jokily say: about my first book *How to become a Multi-Millionaire HMO Landlord* that, "Within seven hours, you'll know as much as I do." So yes, I make it a boast. But it seems to be that the more information you give, the more people come to you. It's perverse.

The whole property world is contradictory. I say to people who come on my courses: "If it doesn't sound right when it comes to property, don't necessarily reject it because it's a topsy-turvy world." The more information I seem to have put out there, the more people seem to come on my courses. I think I have written everything I know about property in my books. But that's often been the case. You don't need to go to university, live in crappy digs, and get drunk every night and whatever else you get up to at university. You can get hold of a reading list and learn by yourself. Nowadays you can sit at home with your computer; it's all there on the Internet.

I find people like the interaction and having things explained to them. All I know is out there — you can read it. I just make it a boast; I don't lose any sleep over it.

I look after my properties and my tenants as a service, because that is my main business and what I'm taking money for. I'm writing books purely for self-satisfaction; I do it as a therapy. The HMO Daddy is more a spin-off of what I do, and I enjoy it. It is like having a well-paid hobby.

What do you do to promote your books, or do you find that readers just find their way to them because they're so hungry for information?

When I give a talk, I'll say: "I've written books," and wave some of them in front of the group, and people buy them.

I sell my manual *How to Become a Multi-Millionaire HMO Landlord* for £597. People may buy it because I say: "This is everything you need to know about being an HMO landlord." I also give them away as part of my courses. Apart from mentioning them on my talks and my website, I do very little else to promote my books. It is something I need to improve.

This is one of the interesting areas in publishing. Because you can package the information as a 5 x 9 paperback. Or, you can publish exactly the same information in a ring-bound folder that changes your readers' perception of it, so this massively increases the price. And, of course, it's still a bargain compared to spending 20 years learning everything that the author has learned ...

Yes, and that's why I've been reluctant to put my first book on Amazon. People sometimes say: "Why don't you publish it and sell it on Amazon?" Well, you'd probably sell it for £30 on Amazon, whereas I have been getting £597 a pop. How many would I have to sell of those, compared to selling them at £30 a pop?

Apparently, it's supposed to get your name out, and it's good for business. But I haven't got a book out there yet that's been on Amazon. Though hopefully I intend to publish a few of my latest books on Amazon soon.

This year I have written five new books: four of them are being edited, and one is sitting around without any publisher though it's been serialised in 'Your Property Network' magazine. The earlier ones I intend to keep as manuals, and I will continue to sell them myself.

You mentioned that you've written books, practical guides if you like, for your children about how to run your business. Have you ever thought of writing children's stories – books to educate children about property, using their kind of language?

No, I haven't thought of writing for children. I think reading bedtime stories to my children has put my children off books for life!

How old are your children now? Have they read your books?

My daughter is eleven, and my two sons are fourteen. They haven't shown much interest in the business yet; I am happy to let them do what they want as long as they do something. Although I have done very well out of property, and it is a fantastic business, it is not the only thing you can do, but with the number of professional people I meet who hate their jobs and want to get into property, I am beginning to wonder.

What type of books do you read yourself?

Whenever I go on a long train journey, I buy two books because they do one for half price. If I read half of one, I've usually done the journey. So I tend to have an enormous amount of books that I've never got around to reading.

I hardly ever read a book: I dip into them. I can't remember the last two I bought. They all tend to be non-fiction. I don't feel I have time to read fiction books. I think it's my Scottish background of feeling you've got to be productive all the time. You've got to spend your time being busy doing something: making money, learning new skills. I've got all Malcolm Gladwell's books; they're really good — *Tipping Point* and *Blink*. The best book I've read lately is *Bad Science* by Ben Goldacre. I try to encourage people to read that, it's an excellent book. It was mind-blowing for me because it reminded me to look for evidence, check the research, but also if you believe it is true it is for you — a bit of a paradox.

When I was young, I read a lot of fiction books. I restarted reading fiction in 2008 when the recession was on. I was sick of property; things were going so badly that I had to relax and switch off, and I started to read fiction again. I read Jeffrey Archer, fantastic writer, and *The Wolf of Wall Street*, which was an excellent book, a well-deserved bestseller. I found there were few others as good. Before that, I've never read a book better than Alistair MacLean's book *HMS Ulysses*. I read that 45 years ago when I was in the merchant navy. That was an absolutely riveting book, mainly because I was in the merchant navy, and it was talking about the Russian convoys. I could just smell it, feel it, and believe it. Strangely enough, I was sailing with a person who had been on the Russian convoy and sunk three times, so it was very realistic to be in that situation.

Normally, I read a book or two in the holidays, but I

haven't this year. It feels like the days are getting shorter and shorter: by the time I get up, it almost seems time to go to bed!

IDEAS FOR YOU

- A book can show your children or staff how your business works; it can improve and promote your brand; it can help you become known as an expert in your field, and it can also be therapy!

- Create spin-off books from the chapters in your first book. Expand upon each chapter to create new, niched books that cover the topics in much greater depth.

- If you use templates for letters, forms or agreements in your property business, consider using these in your book. They will add enormous value to other landlords or property investors.

- If you are running a training course, ask for tips from your attendees or mentees and turn these into a *Book of Tips.*

- The more information you give, the more people will want to work with you or come on your courses.

- One of your selling points for your reader might be: "Within seven hours, you'll know as much as I do!"

- Consider re-packaging your "book" as a ring-bound manual with a premium price.

- A book may sell for £30, but a manual can sell for £597.

- Consider giving your book or manual away as part of a training course to add value to attendees.

DR ROHAN WEERASINGHE

"The great speakers and authors take us on a journey so that we're left with goosebumps..."

Dr Rohan Weerasinghe – a.k.a. Dr Ro – is one of the UK's leading speakers with expertise in property investment, wealth creation and personal development.

He originally followed a traditional path of university education, followed by a career as a civil engineer.

In 2002, together with a business partner, he started to build up an investment portfolio, achieving around 40 properties within a year. This rapidly expanded into other property-related businesses including: rent-to-rent, options, conversions and developments.

Dr Ro started being asked to teach how he achieved his success and has spoken to audiences in over 16

countries. The author of _Turning Point_ is also ambassador for brands such as Robert Kiyosaki's _Rich Dad Education_ and _Making Money from Property_ with BBC television presenter, Martin Roberts.

I grew up in a mixed-race family. My father was Sri Lankan, and my mother was English, and what I didn't know until I was about ten years of age, was that they met under unusual circumstances. It was literally a turning point in my father's life: he had a stroke at twenty-nine and that's when he first met my mother in a multi-let rental property in Birmingham. My father was being taken out on a stretcher at the time.

There were lots of racial challenges at that time in the 1950s and 1960s. My mum fell in love with my father, but in that period it was very difficult to be a white and Asian couple. My mum and dad went through these real ups and downs, eventually moving south with my dad's career. They had three sons, and along the way my father had multiple strokes. At 36, he was paralysed down one side.

I grew up watching my father, who was what would be classified as a disabled man – not that I like the word, but it was a word that was labelled against him. He was a very bright man, but constantly had these mini-setbacks. During that period, my mum just worked and worked and worked during the daytime and had an evening job as well.

So I saw that every day, and I studied very hard. I followed all the rules that were shown to me which meant work hard and pass my academic studies. This was what my father taught me – though ironically, my fathers' qualification (a Masters in Engineering) didn't really help him because of his health. So when I reached the age of 18, I had done enough hard work to get into university and I picked up my first personal development book (which was Ron Hubbard's *Dianetics*). It was my first experience of reading a book that talked about transformational change.

What struck me most was that this book talked about how what a mother thinks and believes affects a baby, and how what we put into our minds affects the results in our lives. This sort of thinking was still relatively new in the 1980s. The personal development world was very much under the radar, read only by a small minority of people. So I read this and got hooked on finding self-help books.

I studied hard for my degree and got my PhD. But there were always setbacks along the way. My father died when I was thirteen years of age, which was a big shift in my family. My father was a Buddhist so we had his ashes scattered, but we still had a ceremony for him. My uncles and aunties put their hands on my shoulders and said: "You've got to be successful. You're the head of the family now: you're responsible." They were just little things that came out of their mouths, but because they were linked to such a significant emotional event, which was my father's passing and funeral, I got it in my head that I had to be successful, look after my family and be this protector.

So I went all the way through the process of becoming successful, because I believed that was how I was going to solve the problems for my mother. Having got my PhD, the company I then went to work for streamlined me into becoming a director of the company as a civil engineer. Meanwhile, I was still reading these personal development books by authors like Tony Robins, Wayne Dyer, Jim Rohn and Les Brown, and broadening my horizons.

I got involved with a network marketing business back in

the 1980s, Amway Corporation. In those days, it was one of the first network marketing businesses that came into the country. It was a powerful experience because it got me speaking in front of audiences for the first time. It was all the books that came with this that really opened my eyes. I loved the concept of books that I could read maybe a sentence that would strike a chord and move me to tears or just wake me up in the morning and I'd think, "Fuck, I'm just going to do this now." It definitely had an impact on me. I knew that the written word could make a huge difference.

So you felt that you had your own book inside you. Though you didn't write a traditional property book: you drew on your own experiences and journey. Tell me more about that.

I knew there were lots of books inside me: I had this feeling for years, "I've got a book inside me; I've got a book inside me." When it came to the time to write, I thought, 'Let me ask a few people what they think I should write about.' Many people said, "You've got to write about wealth or property. You've got your portfolio and you've helped thousands of people do the same – that's the foundation of your book." The more I thought about it, I felt that the real foundation was mindset. Actually, that is my foundation because my whole background, my PhD, was foundation engineering. I wanted a book that would help people *re-engineer* their lives.

Any building has to sit on a strong foundation. Whether it's a house or whether it's an eighty-storey building. The walls of the basement have to be reinforced, and the foundations have to be reinforced, and all of the weight of the structure then sits on that foundation.

70

So I started to look at why I'd succeeded maybe more than some of the people who I thought were brighter than me, and it all went back to the foundations. It went back to the three elements that I talk about in my book, which are: understanding the *foundations* of the building which is your life; looking at the *structure* which is how you show up in your life; and looking at the architecture or the *blueprint*, which is the vision of your life.

All three things must be aligned. For example, there are thousands of people who think they can fix their life by going out and building property portfolios. But that's like trying to say: "I want to fix the windows of my house," without realising that the brickwork has deteriorated, the roof's leaking, and the house is sitting over the top of an old mineshaft. So the house is sinking and this is what's causing the brickwork to break up and the windows to crack. So people try to fix the *structure* of their life without realizing it's the *foundation* that needs to be fixed.

When I wrote the *Turning Point*, I thought, 'You know what: we need to start at the base.' I wanted to give people something so that they could have a tool that they could apply into wealth, health and their daily lives. *Turning Point* was really born from my own personal journey and my experience helping other people.

Whenever I have a conversation, something personal always comes out which is a transformation. For example, I get Mr and Mrs Jones, in the room (whether it's a personal development event or a property event) and he says, "Gosh, my wife was made redundant a year and half ago. She's not been able to get another job and my employer is now talking about downsizing. We need to do something different." I'll say to them, "Well, you're going through a turning point. Literally, something is happening to you right now, and if we talk in two years you'll have taken a different direction. We need to address the direction right now rather than wait for two years." So *Turning Point* evolved because I believe that most people wait for something to happen to them instead of taking active, conscious decisions to change their direction.

My life has definitely been changed by people who have inspired me through personal development, and I wanted that to be the first message that came from the book.

So tell me about the process while you were writing your book. Was it easy to fit it in around your property business?

When I started the process of thinking about the book and writing notes, it was very drawn out – about three years initially. Then I made a decision that it had to be done fast and effectively. So I sat back, and I thought, 'I don't want to drag this out. I've got a really powerful message I want to get across, so I need to apply the same techniques that I do in other areas of my life to get a result here.' So I put aside two hours a day for a six-week period and I made a promise to Savannah, my daughter (who at the time was two-and-a-half years of age), that by the end of the year Daddy would have written a book and that would be my gift to her. So I chose 2011 to be the year that the book would be published and I literally blocked out a six-week period.

I remember listening to Bob Proctor talk about "The 6am Club" many years ago. I think he wrote his first book by getting up at 6am and putting in a couple of hours before everybody else got up. Usually, I work best in either the early hours or the late part of the day. I like the peace and quiet of the sun rising at 5am and I have a habit of starting at 10pm and going right through to 2am or 3am, which allows me to focus. I tended to put music on in the background that didn't have words; so it was light jazz, classical music, or Spanish guitar. That would just play in the background and was like white noise to me – that gave me something comfortable to get into a space.

Explain more about how you plotted out your book.

I started with a mind map. I've been studying mind maps for thirty odd years now. So for me it was a natural process to capture everything. So I mind-mapped the entire book: I isolated the key subjects that I wanted to cover, and these became chapters. I then went into each of these subjects, really deciding what the message was.

For me, the book had to be about the message. I didn't want it to be a lightweight book that people just flicked through quickly and said, "Yeah, that's quite good". I wanted each chapter to have depth behind it. Then, I filtered that down to what the key messages were for each chapter and how I wanted to get these across. I did that chapter by chapter.

About six years ago, when I had the first idea for a book, I tried to flit around and jump in and out of chapters. That didn't work. So this time, I worked all the way through in a logical sequence from the front to the back of the book. I must have spent two weeks just preparing the structure, nothing else. I didn't try writing anything as that was the mistake I made before.

Yes, that's a very typical mistake.

So just two solid weeks of preparation. If there were ideas, I would just quickly jot them down and they'd be mind-mapped. So it was big picture first. Each chapter was put on one central mind map, and each chapter was put as a central thing in its own mind map. I've still got them here. They would pan out into the details of each chapter; coming down two or three levels into the mind map.

When I started to write, I didn't have to think. All the right-brain creativity had been done already. That was the biggest mistake I'd made when I started playing with the idea of writing a book years back. I was flipping between left and right brain constantly. "Oh, great I've got an idea. I can put it in there," then I'd try to write it, and, of course it didn't flow. So this was very much creativity first: right brain, big picture, get the mind map set out. Then it was, "OK, now let's move into the left brain, just laying out the chapters." So that allowed me to put it on the wall in front of me.

When I got my computer out, there were no distractions while I typed. I was pretty strict. After about two hours, I would stop. If I was absolutely in a flow, and there was nobody around, I would keep going for another hour, and it was done in six weeks.

A great strategy for anyone who has to fit in writing around a business. Tell me about how you came up with your title.

I brainstormed a bunch of title ideas. I knew it had to be no more than two words. One of the things I've learned over the years is that if you keep it simple, people tend to remember it. I know there are exceptions to that and I read some amazing books that have longer titles. But for me personally, I just wanted it to be simple. So having written the book first, the title didn't emerge until the end of it.

I had lots of different ideas to do with foundations,

structures and transformation. Then, I went to bed one night and I meditated. I lay there in bed and started to picture messages. I just put it out there that "I want to come up with an idea that feels the most comfortable and natural to me." I went to bed thinking about a journey, which was what the book was about. When I woke up, it was about 3 a.m. or 4 a.m. I always keep a little journal beside the bed and I just wrote down *Turning Point*. It just struck me that this book was about lots of turning points. I went out to about ten different people and asked, "What are your thoughts on these three titles?" – *Turning Point* was one of them. Virtually everyone came back and said, "That's it. That's the one: *Turning Point*."

Everyone that I speak to, if you have enough of a conversation with them, somewhere in there they'll talk to you about tipping points or a turning point. I use this reference a lot when people have had a traumatic experience and are caught between making a decision. We had a lady at one of our events last year. Her husband was in bed with somebody else, and it was an absolute kick in the face for her. She came to the event and she was distraught. I said, "Well OK, let's take this as a turning point. What's come out of this? How have you grown from this?" At once she shifted. It is a metaphor. So the book was really picking it up and saying, "I'm ready for a turning point. This is a conscious chance to make a turning point in my life." That's how it evolved really.

What sort of impact has writing a book had – both on your own life and on your readers' lives?

I think on a personal level – and I know from the great work that you do – it definitely gives the person who has written the book a sense of personal gratification. If we have something that we're passionate about, it's our destiny to fulfil it. For me, writing the book was one hundred per cent that. It was about getting out a message that was bursting inside of me. As much as I love speaking to an audience, you can speak to a hundred people, but a book can impact thousands more lives. So on a personal level, you achieve a sense of being able to give back or leave a legacy for years to come. From a business perspective, a book is also your calling card. I usually carry a couple of copies of my book with me, and if someone touches my life, it's a simple gesture to give them the book.

There was a lady at an airport a couple of years ago; I think I was flying out to Singapore. There was a lady checking me in and I was talking to her, just general conversation. She was having a bit of a tough week. Her mum had found out that she was pretty ill with health-related issues. I said, "I'd like to share something with you." I just gave her a book and I signed it. I said, "You don't have to read the whole book, but there's a chapter in there that talks about health. My mother went through a similar journey and there might be one or two messages in here that might help you get a message across to your mother." That was a great feeling of being able to do something, and to know that I wasn't doing it for recognition, but to give somebody a message that I couldn't get across in those two or three minutes while I've got a bunch of other people standing behind me in the airport. That's happened so many times over the last three years since I've written the book.

So on a personal level what a book does is it gives you exposure. It allows you to be able to say, "I'm an author" and say it with pride, and it's given me the opportunity to pick up the phone and speak with people like you. For example, I was in India a month ago and the BBC radio said, "Dr Rohan we'd like to do an interview with you on relationships. We know you've got a whole chapter on it, and we've seen your work, so we'd like to do an interview with you and get your thoughts about couples breaking up during a recession."

The book has to be written with a strong message to start with. The message has to be pure. It has to be authentic. It needs to be something that you know is going to touch people's lives in a positive way. When you do that, it will reach places you just wouldn't expect. I've been into countries, been on the stage, and somebody has come up and said they've got the Kindle version of my book and I'm like "Wow!" It's a lovely feeling to be going around the world and knowing that people are reading your work.

So I think there are three things. Firstly, personal gratification. Secondly, the fact that it can raise your profile as an author or speaker. And thirdly, it's a great tool for a person to be able to use with audiences. I've spoken recently to a company – it's a multi-level marketing type business – they have a lot of people in their organization. They liked the message that the book had, and so they asked if they could buy about one hundred and fifty copies for a particular audience they wanted me to speak to. So every member of the audience got a copy of the book and I was able to sign the books. It has also raised my profile in the corporate environment as well, and that's been happening now for three years.

In terms of the change in other people's lives, I think you could go so far as to say they are immeasurable. Here's a random story: I walked into a café with my business partner and his family about six days ago. We'd been out for a beautiful walk, and we went into a café to have a cup of tea and give the kids a treat. In the room in the café, was a family that I'd spoken in front of in 2014, and the lady came up to me and said, "Dr Rohan, I read your book, and I just loved the section on health and relationships." Her husband and son were there, and he started talking to me too. So there were three people who I'd seen months before in a random audience, and she was coming up and sharing something that she had taken from my book.

I think the great thing about writing a book is that the person reading it can consciously and unconsciously process what you're writing – your message to them, privately – whether they're on the loo, whether they're on the train or at home. What I've found is that people can process *Turning Point* because it's quite deep, as you know. It's a transformational book, and they can go through a shift in a private way, which they wouldn't necessarily do in a more public environment. Being so open in the book has allowed people to read it and it's almost given them permission to say, "OK, I need to let go of this or make this change. He talked about this and it's OK for me to do this."

I think the book has allowed people to overcome some of the blocks or the resistance they have in the normal environment, because the way I've written it is like a conversation between me and the person reading it. My intention, when I wrote *Turning Point*, was for it to be my voice rather than a "This is how you do it" type of voice. It's about trying to capture the experience of being in a room with me saying, "Hey listen, you're in a good place and it's OK. We can go through this together." Does that make sense?

Yes. Brian Tracy [author of *Eat That Frog*] put it very well when I interviewed him for my last book. He said he writes as if he's talking intimately one on one, rather than speaking to a stadium full of people – which is what first-time authors often do.

Yes, that's very true. The challenge that I had was that the book itself was probably one and a half times the thickness of what it is now. I tend to be a storyteller, so that had to change. The book was great, but I didn't want it to be so big that people wouldn't want to make their way through it. Sometimes, I'll open a book, and it almost feels likes somebody's writing because they have to pop something in there. Whereas when we're writing, we need to put something in that has enough depth in it for the reader to take the intellectual side of the writing and to emotionalise it. That is a skill. If the author can take a message from the left brain, and then emotionalise it, that is such a gift. I think the great speakers and authors are the people that take us on a journey so that we're left with goosebumps, which I'm getting while I'm talking to you now. So maybe my message is right. It has to be a feeling that somebody has when they turn the page or close the book.

I agree totally. Tell me about what you did to promote your book when it came out.

The launch was at a conference with three hundred people there. So I was able to talk about *Turning Point* and to pick two areas from the book. So it was promoted as: How to Create a Transformational Turning Point in Your Life. That was the title they put as my speech. So I think we printed around three hundred books ahead of the event, and I put the intention out there. I said, "Right, we're going to go there and get these books into three hundred people's lives." I didn't just want people in the audience to take a book but to buy a copy and take a copy for someone they knew. So part of my theme on stage was, "How many of you are going through a transformation or a turning point or have had something happen to you recently that you know you could do some work on? Then, by a show of hands, how many of you know somebody else who is going through something similar?" That's what gets a live audience engaged with the promotion of a book. I know people don't like talking about selling. The English are a bit cautious about the word "selling." But ultimately when we're writing a book, we want to sell the book because we want it to get into the hands of people who are going to get the benefit from it.

Authors need to be comfortable with promoting their work. They've put all these hours in. You know: the late nights, the reading, the proofreading, the reviewing, and all those hours going into preparation. And then, what I've seen over the years is that people get to the hurdle of promotion and their voice suddenly goes very quiet. So their voice is loud on paper but quiet in the arena of promotion. Wouldn't you agree?

Yes, the majority of authors struggle with promoting themselves and their books. They don't like blowing their own trumpet.

I think we have to be equally as loud verbally and in the social media environment or wherever we are out in the real world as we are on the paper. So I made that decision. I said, "I'm going to be proud of what I've done." I brought my family with me. My fiancé and my daughter were on this desk where we had all the books. I went on stage and did maybe 90 minutes, with lots of hard content. I brought people onto the stage because it's an interventional process with a turning point. I took them through a couple of the examples, and during the process of talking had copies of the book on the stage. So I got people to take down the page number of the work we were doing. I'd say, "We're working on this particular area right now. I'll cover one or two points with you, but as you can see here on page X, there is a section on beliefs." There were lots of questions because people were putting their hands up. So I'd say, "If you go into the chapter, there are a whole bunch of questions you can use to work on yourself or your partner or whoever you're working with". So what that led to was people immediately being engaged with wanting to look at the book.

Anyone can do this to promote a book, even if you're not a fantastic speaker or you're not a skilled speaker. You *can* talk about something passionately, and your book is what you're passionate about. So whether it's writing about pets or real estate or business or health, just find an organization or group that's passionate about that and tell them you'd like to come and share a section of what you've written about in your book. That gives them a window into what you're talking about. This is what I did. I said, "Look, I've got copies of my book over there and I will leave when the last person leaves and I'll sign every book that you buy. My suggestion is that we'll give a special offer: we'll give two books for a discounted price." I was encouraging people to take a book away and give it as a gift. So we sold out completely at that event. It was amazing. That was the very first launch of the book.

Excellent. Tell me about the book that you're writing now. That's a different style of book, isn't it?

The current book is a property-related book. That's been in the making now for probably longer than *Turning Point*. I don't want to make the book a standard nuts and bolts and "how to" property book. There are some amazing books out there already. The subject is well written about, although there's always space for more. It's a cross-over between personal development, wealth development and property investing – that's the essence of the book. The book is taking the reader on a journey. It's not really aimed at sophisticated, experienced investors, although there are always tools in every book that people can use. It's more geared at people coming into property or who have been in property a little while who are possibly going through some blocks.

I've been in front of, I guess, hundreds of thousands of people over the last twelve years as a property speaker and there seem to be three levels of people. There are those that are brand new. There are those who've bought a few properties but seem to have hit a block, and then there are the very experienced ones. The way I've structured the book is for it to be a journey like *Turning Point*. It's not a heavy read, so that people can go through it and reference different sections. So it's going to cover communication and negotiation – I think that's an area that's not covered enough in real estate. It's about understanding, especially when buying a house, how to communicate in a way that makes this a win-win for yourself and them. So it's very much about getting into the psychology of working with sellers and the people in your power team.

It's also about walking the reader through the numbers, which I know you may not pick up from this conversation, but I'm very much a left-brain numbers person. So, whether you're brand new or experienced, you can refine your existing property business by taking these tools and I literally walk them through the process of overcoming the mental blocks, overcoming the issues such as how to look for money and how to look at property. I show them how to walk into the property market in a way that's graceful, so they don't chase the deals and chase the money, but make it a journey. That's the message I really want to get across.

I also deal with the emotional blocks that can stop people, which I'm sure you come across yourself with entrepreneurs where people are coming out of job mindsets into entrepreneur mindsets. So my book tackles this block that I come across for a lot of people which is, "I'm in a job right now but I want to get into a real estate business, and learn how to take the discipline of it being a job and mixing it with the skill and creativity of being an entrepreneur." That's not an easy transition. Books like *The E Myth Revisited* by Michael Gerber do a very good job, but that's more about business whereas I've tailored this for property. It will cover even simple things like: how do I set my property business up? Should I be a sole trader or a limited company? Mortgages; basic stuff. It's about knowing how to do it quickly and efficiently, rather than shopping around for it and having a coaching call. I'm going to have things in there like questions for negotiating, and when you're dealing with an estate agent or a solicitor. It's going to be a reasonably comfortable light read, rather than a detailed lots-of-spreadsheets type of book. But at the same time, it will be something that people can keep as a reference source, as well.

You use metaphors a lot to get your message across in a powerful way. Explain more about this...

Yes, let's look at the theme of human re-engineering and bring it into context with property investing, for example. If we take the three elements – the *foundation*, the *structure* and the *architecture* – and we can imagine that in each area of your life you've got these three elements.

In property, for the people reading this book right now, the *foundations* of your property investing business on a personal development level include your beliefs about your capabilities to build a property business; your beliefs about whether you can raise money; your beliefs about whether you're going to get support from your partner and your family; beliefs about whether you have the ability to build enough properties in your portfolio to become financially independent. I know these may sound simple, but to some people they are huge blocks. These are foundational beliefs, and if you don't work on them, then you can work as hard as you want on doing a cash flow calculation or renovating a property and get nowhere. I've seen people self-destruct because they get to a certain point and the structure they're building is too heavy for the foundations of their own personal beliefs. They collapse and they go back into self-destructive patterns.

So *foundations* also include values about integrity. You have to decide as a property investor how you want to operate. What values do you have and how do you want them to align with the people you're working with? I won't do business with other people unless I know, from talking to them, that their values align with mine. For example: honesty, integrity and wanting to give back. If you're doing a joint venture with somebody, do they want to keep all the money and you want to give ten per cent to charity? Those values are foundational values and need to align with the people you're working with. When you're going into property business, it's really important to get the foundations straight.

The *structure* of your property business includes money management. If you're going to have money coming in, have separate accounts set up and make sure everything is traceable. Make sure you have the right legal teams in place. Have the right power team around you to make that business work. Another structure to your business is fund-raising. These are the practical elements.

The last part of the human re-engineering to property is *architecture*. This is the blueprint. No matter what time of the year it is, you're always looking ahead to the future. The start of the year is usually a good time to do this. You look at your property business and say, "This year I'd like to add another ten properties to my business," or "This year I'd like to add another £5,000 a month passive income to my business," or, "This year I'd like to have another thirty tenants in my property business", or "I'd like to buy and sell five properties this year." This is the big picture now. "The reason I want to do that is because at the end of the year I'm going to use some of that profit to take my family on a holiday or move home." There has to be a purpose behind your property business and every property you buy. I think what's very powerful is to give each property a purpose and to give your overall business a purpose as well.

If you tie these three elements together, you have: the big picture which you should review monthly; the practical day-to-day that should be reviewed weekly; and the foundations which should have on-going monitoring. These three elements in harmony will build you a very successful and profitable property business that's going to help a lot of people in the future.

IDEAS FOR YOU

- Give your readers tools they can apply in their wealth, health and daily lives.

- Set aside two hours a week over a six-week period and promise to finish your book in this time.

- Start with a mind map for your entire book. Isolate the key subjects you want to cover, then decide on your key message in each chapter.

- Don't try writing your book until you are happy with the structure.

- Keep your book title simple and people will remember it. Test out your title ideas on different people and ask for feedback.

- Meditate before going to sleep, and keep a journal by your bed to jot down ideas when you wake.

- Use metaphors to get your message across in a powerful way.

- Being open about your own transformations will help others overcome their own blocks.

- Use your own personal voice rather than a "how to" voice. Write as if it's a conversation with your reader.

- Carry a couple of your books around with you. If someone touches your life, give them a copy.

- Encourage your audience to buy a book and give a copy to someone else they know.

- Be comfortable with promoting your book on social media and in the real world. Your confident voice on paper should be just as loud off paper!

- Find a group that's passionate about your topic and ask if you can come along and share a section from your book.

- Engage your audience by showing transformations on stage that involve chapters from your book.

- Offer to sign every book that's bought ... and promise not to leave until they're all signed.

JOHN LEE

"Now, I've got people paying me £10,000 to £15,000 a day just because I'm a speaker and an author."

Self-made property millionaire John Lee is a world-class speaker who has shared the stage with the likes of Sir Richard Branson, former US President Bill Clinton, Sir Alan Sugar, James Caan and Anthony Robbins.

He is director and co-founder of Wealth Dragons Ltd and author of books including *Property Millionaire Secrets* and *A Step-by-Step Guide to Lease Options.*

He rose from humble beginnings working in a Chinese takeaway, and overcame dyslexia, to later building a multi-million pound property portfolio within three years.

His latest book *The Wealth Dragons Way* is published by Wiley.

My latest book is called *The Wealth Dragon Way* — it's about giving people a financial education so they can do what they want to do. Right now, people go to school, they get a job and they make a living; they get trained through many years to be good at something and to trade their time for money. Well, people don't have to do that. People can create a vehicle where it makes money for them. They have to spend time building that vehicle. But once that vehicle is done, then it will pay them money every single month.

The book talks about how I was able to do that using the vehicle of property. So I go through my story of how I was able to buy a lot of houses very quickly, and even when finance got a little bit scarce, how I was still able to grow that portfolio. Now we have three property companies around the world and all doing very well.

So you blended your personal story with factual information. Did you feel uncomfortable with exposing your personal life in that way or were you quite comfortable with that?

No, I was quite comfortable with that. In the book, I talk about how I lose money as well. There's a strategy for losing money and there's a strategy for earning money. If you use the strategy that I did back then, or any of the strategies that I warn you about, then you're going to lose money. You see, most books are very fluffy. They kind of *tell* you, but don't really *tell* you anything. I wanted to write a book that would inspire you but also get you started. This was one of the biggest frustrations for me when I started. I'd read a book, but then after the book: "So what do I do? What is there?" There is often nothing else. A book often kind of leaves you hanging.

My message is: if someone like me can do it, you can too. I

wasn't the most intelligent guy, and I struggle with learning. I'm dyslexic, and I find it very hard to read. I'm not intellectually intelligent at all. But I want to give people the belief that anyone can do it. Most people are a lot smarter than I am, you know.

So if I can do it, they can do it. I wanted to inspire others with my story and I also wanted to lay out the truth of what it's like. Everyone makes it sound so easy: it's simple, but it's not easy. So I wanted to show that when I started, it was a struggle. It was a struggle because I didn't have these elements in place, and when I figured out what the elements were, then my journey was a lot quicker. So when people read the book, they're not only being inspired by "Hey, if I can do it you can do it," but also I give them a step-by-step strategy that they can implement. Then, I also tell them about the result I got when I implemented the strategy. So it's tangible. It's not just like airy-fairy fluffy stuff.

Your first book was self-published. Your latest book is published by Wiley. Why did you decide to go with a mainstream publisher rather than self-publishing this time around?

One thing I learnt from the first time around is that: "I'm not a writer, I'm dyslexic!" In fact, that book had many spelling mistakes in it, and the grammar wasn't correct either. When Vince [co-author Vincent Wong] and I co-wrote that book, it was just something that people kept asking us about. So we said, "Look, let's just write a book." I wrote half of the book and Vince wrote half of the book, and then we kind of just pasted it together, and I have to say, that book is not a well-written book at all. But it's not about how well it's written; what's important is what people get from it. People have read that book and have made a *lot* of money. A lot of people come up to me and say: "Oh my God, I read your book about lease options, and it was amazing, I just bought this first house and made £25,000. Wow!"

So it wasn't grammatically written and it didn't look professional, but for all that, it served its purpose. So we wanted to go with a publisher because of the perceived professionalism. To start with, I thought that it would be good to have a professional publisher because they could take care of the marketing and they could do all the promotion. Little did I know that really, all they're doing is just putting their stamp and their name on the book. They're not really doing the other stuff. So I went with a publisher because I wanted the book to look more professional, because sometimes when you self publish, you don't get that finished professional touch. It looks like a book but it looks like a home-made, high quality book if that makes sense.

With the first book, you used videos a lot to market yourself and your book. Tell me more about that and how you went about the marketing process using YouTube?

It's funny because when YouTube came out many years ago, I was one of the first adopters, I guess. What I started to realize was that I wasn't very good at writing, and my spelling mistakes were really bad, and my emails were really bad. So I just thought, 'What's the easiest way to do this without sounding stupid?' I put a camera up because I thought, 'Well, people won't judge me based on my spelling now.' So I just put the video up with me talking about the book. I said, "You know, this book is about how you can invest in property using cutting edge strategies. Everything you've been told about property is wrong, and you don't have to use money to buy property. You can use leverage to buy property."

So I put that video up. Within a day, I'd already had close to five hundred views, and then the next day I had a thousand views. Now, some of my videos have got thousands and thousands and thousands of views. When I did that I thought, 'Wow, maybe people do watch this stuff!" Then people would make comments, "Oh my God, that's really interesting," and "You talk about Chapter Seven, but I don't have your book. Where can I buy your book?" I started to realize that, "Wow, people watch the video and it actually gets them interested in the book. So maybe I should make another video."

So I spent a little bit more time on the next one and I made it a little bit more professional. I bought some lamps and I got a white background. I wore a shirt and I got a haircut, and I tried to look a little bit more professional. I filmed the video and again: ten views … twenty views … one hundred views … two hundred views … five hundred … a thousand … two thousand … five thousand. It just kept growing and growing and growing.

I thought, 'Wow, people really do watch videos!' When I did some research, I discovered that people like to educate themselves by watching a video because it takes a lot less effort. Its consumption is a lot easier than reading a whole book or attending a workshop. What I noticed is that whenever I made the videos between one and five minutes, people would watch it all the way to the end. I also noticed that any time they'd be over an hour, people would never watch it. I quickly realized that if I'm making a video, what actually happens is, that it creates intrigue. When you create intrigue, people go, "Wow, maybe I should pick this book up." So that's what I learnt from making videos.

Another thing I learnt is that people would watch the video, and they would invite me to speak at a property event without even knowing who I was. They just saw a video of me presenting and they thought, "Let's get this guy to speak at my event.' A funny thing then happened when I turned up at the event. I had all these people started coming to me: "Oh my God, you're John Lee. Oh my God, you're that guy with that book. It was like I almost had this celebrity status: I became a *somebody*. What started to happen is that people would come up to me and then ask me questions that even I didn't know the answer to. I said: "Why are you asking me that? I'm just a property investor, why are you asking me? I'm not a tax adviser!" What I learned from that was, the moment you create a video is the moment you become a celebrity, is the moment you can sell more books.

So true. So tell me about your strategy for driving traffic to your videos. Did you use Pay Per Click campaigns?

I just put the first video on YouTube and then it started getting a lot of traction. The thing with YouTube is that there are different algorithms that you can use to cause your video to rank highly. SEO, or search engine optimization, is how you optimize the words, so you can use this, for example. A friend of mine, he's a wedding photographer in Manchester, and he said, "I've got this really cool website and I'm not getting much business." So I did a search for 'wedding photographer' and found out that he was on page two of Google. People don't really look at page two — only a very small percentage of people go past page one — so he was losing out on a lot of the traffic for organic searches.

So on applying this learning to YouTube, what I realized

was that people don't look for *you*, they look for what *they* are looking for. One of the biggest videos that really worked for me was '*How To Get Deals From Estate Agents*' and that's how I named the video. Most people would name the video, '*John Lee: Video Property Expert*', but that's not what people are looking for. People wouldn't type in '*John Lee Property Expert.*' They type in exactly what they're looking for, which is '*how to get deals from estate agents.*' So when they type that in, it's what we call a long-tail key word, and YouTube optimizes your key words, your body tags, your links, your descriptions and also the relevancy of the video of how many times it's watched. So if it gets a lot of attraction really quickly at any one time, YouTube notices. Also, another thing I started finding is that people would reply to the video and say: "Hey John, that didn't quite make sense" or, "You know, it doesn't sound like you can do that."

So I'd go back and reply, which was actually a mistake looking back at it. But what happened is that the more interaction you have on the video comments, the more it pushes the video up the rankings and the more relevant it becomes. Google and YouTube go, "Wow, people are really commenting on this." It doesn't matter if there are negative comments like: "Oh no, I don't believe you can do this" because then someone will come back and say: "Of course you can." So when you create a kind of debate, it creates a lot of traction; a lot of replies go out and then it appears on other social media at the same time. This all makes your video relevant and, therefore, it ranks higher. If your video ranks higher, it gets more views, then people get more interested and they buy more books.

You use other social media, such as Facebook, a lot to sell your books and to promote your business as well. Tell me more about your strategy for an effective

campaign on social media.

Well, I think it's really important because people know who you are, but they don't know who you are! What I mean by this is: when people hear about your book, they'll immediately search for you. So if you don't have a Facebook account or a YouTube account or a Twitter account, forget it. You're not important. So when you're on social media, it's important that you have the right image. So with my Facebook, it's not a picture of me in a T-shirt, it's a picture of me in a suit and tie, with a nice, professional profile picture. All your pictures need to describe what you do. So my pictures are all about events, education, lifestyle, charity, giving back and self-education.

All my stuff on Facebook is about that. Sometimes I'll show pictures of events, sometimes I'll show pictures of what's going on in my life. For example, if I'm flying on a plane, I'll take a picture of me in First Class, I'll post it on there, and I'll make a comment. Sometimes if I'm on a beach and I'm working with my laptop, I'll take a picture of that. The social media has to be congruent with what your message is and what your book is about. That's really important.

Here's another thing. If you go to Twitter and you type in something like *'property investor'* and you find John Lee versus someone else, and you find that John Lee has got seventy thousand followers and another high-profile person has only got a hundred followers, that doesn't look good.

So your congruency has to go through everything. My YouTube channel has got something like 2.7 million views. It's not a lot, but it's a lot for the niche. So when you have social media, all your social media profiles have to match. If you go to LinkedIn, I've been endorsed 99 plus for almost every sector. So when people look me up, they see that I have a massive following on Facebook and Twitter, then on YouTube they see I've got millions of people watching. Then, if they check LinkedIn, they see loads of people have endorsed me and I've got thousands of connections there.

As long as you continually update, social media is really great for building relationships and being in people's minds. So when you're on Facebook, for example, when you're posting stuff all the time and people consistently see you posting stuff, they don't necessarily respond. But it's there in the background and they see it. So it's not necessarily about selling, but about being at the top of people's minds.

What about your tips for selling *bundles* of books? Obviously that's every author's ideal: not just to sell one book to one person, but 50 books at a time, or a hundred books at a time. Do you have any tips for selling books in bulk?

Yes, absolutely. One of the things that you've got to remember is that people always buy the package or bundle. It's like when you go into Tesco or IKEA or whatever shop you go into, you always end up buying like 'two for one' or 'three for two' deals. You never really use the third one or even need it. Sometimes the deal isn't even that much cheaper, but you buy it because you buy the package.

So when you're positioning a single product versus a bundle, packages always sell better than a single product. The funny thing is that I've even sold bundles where, if they'd have bought the book and other items separately, it might have been a lot cheaper. But they bought the bundle because they thought there was more value in the bundle.

So when you're thinking of selling bundles, or when you've packaged something together, you've got to ask, "What do people want?" When you know this, then you think, 'What's the fastest thing that they can do right now to get that end result?' The moment they can get a package that delivers the end result, then people will buy the bundled package every time.

Great. What sort of impact has having a book had on your business? Once you've written one book, why write another?

You've always got to be seen to be doing something. It's a bit like speaking when you're standing on a stage. Even if you don't know what you're talking about, people assume you know what you're talking about because you're standing on stage. The moment you're an author and you keep writing books, again even if you're not the best person to teach that subject, the book makes you the best person to teach that subject. So it's had a huge impact because the more books I write the more credibility I get.

Here's another thing I found out as well: if you're an author, you charge more. Before I wrote a book and before I was a speaker, I was charging £1,000 per day and that's still a lot to some people. But now, I've got people paying me £10,000 to £15,000 a day, just because I'm a speaker and an author. They read my books and then they get star-struck. They're like: "Oh my God, you're that author and you're that speaker as well. You spoke to thousands of people with Richard Branson and Bill Clinton. It's like wow!"

So the reason we keep writing books is to carry on building our profile, so that people see us in the position in the market that we want to be in.

How does it work when you're actually co-authoring a book with Vince? Is it more complicated to co-author a book or do you find it more rewarding?

I think co-authoring is good because it gives you two different perspectives. Sometimes with a book, it's about the one person writing it, it's all about them and their perspective. It's interesting when two people are delivering the same message. The way of doing it might seem a little bit like *Karate Kid*, you know, "Mr Miyagi, I don't know why I'm doing this wax-on, wax-off thing, it doesn't make sense." But at the end, we both end up in the same destination. So I think, especially for the latest book, *The Wealth Dragon Way*, Vincent and I became very wealthy in property, but we got there through different paths. So we have two very different examples and walking testimonies of how one guy was already wealthy to start with and he was on a £100K salary and one guy was working in a Chinese takeaway as a dishwasher, but yet they both ended up in the same place.

So is it a lot harder to write? Absolutely, because you're duplicating content and you have to teach different content. But I think in terms of getting your names out there and building a brand, now you have two people to promote the book. So when you talk about marketing and promoting, you've got a Vincent Wong funnel and a John Lee funnel, which both have their fan bases driving into one place. That means you have two fan bases to sell one book. So you get more sales.

Is your strategy for promoting and marketing your books mainly done online? Or do you have an offline marketing strategy too?

Most of it is online. Offline, we have a Wealth Dragons

Ambassador Program and our ambassadors actually go out and spread the word for us. Our other offline strategy is when people come to our events: they can buy the books at the event in bundles, or if they sign up for a programme, we give them five extra books for free. Then they are asked to change five other people's lives by giving them books. But mainly, our strategy is online.

The set-up for online can be done offline. So I might meet with someone who is a strategic alliance partner and I'll have dinner with them. I'll give them massive value and I'll do this six months before my launch, so I know that when my launch comes I've done them a favour and, of course, they'll be doing me a favour.

So offline, I meet people with big networks, big lists, and I try to help them in any way I can. Then when I come to ask for a favour, nine times out of ten they don't mind helping. So most of our promotion and marketing really is about list building, online product launching, social media, paid advertising, that kind of stuff. We don't really do so much offline.

In the past when you've spoken at my events, you've talked about getting competitors to sell your books. Tell me more about getting competitors to sell your books.

It's interesting because, funnily enough, I just had a competitor call me on Skype recently. He's one of my biggest competitors, and he said to me: "John, will you help me launch my book?" and I said, "Well, why would I do that?" He said: "Well, if you help me launch my book, then I may help you launch your book." The way you've got to look at it is this: we're in an industry of abundance and buyers will always be buyers. Buyers will buy from me and buyers will buy from my competitors, and the buyers that don't buy from my competitors will buy from me. So the way we see it is, it benefits both of you to promote for each other. It's always got to be a win-win.

IDEAS FOR YOU

- Many books are inspirational but don't tell readers the nuts and bolts of what they need to do. Give your readers step-by-step strategies.

- Mainstream publishers don't take care of all the marketing and promotion. This is still the author's responsibility.

- Create videos to generate a buzz around your book and put them up on YouTube. People often hire you to speak after they've watched you presenting.

- Keep videos between one and five minutes maximum. People rarely watch videos over an hour.

- Don't use your author name and book title on your YouTube description. Instead, ask yourself what topics your readers are likely to be looking for and use these keywords as your description.

- Encourage people to leave comments on your video to help push it up the rankings.

- It's important to have the right image on social media. Consider whether you should be wearing a T-shirt or a suit and tie.

- Your postings on social media should tie in with your message and your book. All your pictures and postings should reinforce this message.

- Update social media, such as Facebook, Twitter or LinkedIn, regularly in order to stay at the top of people's minds.

- Consider how to create a package with your books. People love to buy 'two for one' and 'three for two' deals.

- When you're thinking of selling bundles of books, ask, "What do people want?" Give them what they want rather than what you think they need.

- Two authors are sometimes better than one! Co-authoring has the advantage of giving you two different perspectives on your topic. You will also have two fan bases to sell your book.

VICKI WUSCHE

"What you need with a book launch is a 'Ta-daaa!' date."

Vicki Wusche is author of three 'do-it-yourself' property books and has recently been named as one of the UK's top twenty-five most influential people in property by *The Daily Telegraph.*

She bought her first rental property six years ago. Since then, she has become a buy-to-let evangelist, criss-crossing the country, giving motivational speeches and holding workshops to help other people find success the same way. Her mantra is: "If I can do it, so can you."

Over recent years, Vicki has shifted her focus from personal property investing to creating two successful property businesses through sourcing property and training others. She is known throughout the industry as The Property Mermaid because of her lifelong passion for scuba diving.

She has written and spoken on property and business matters in publications including *The Telegraph, The Observer, The Daily Express, What Mortgage* and *Business Matters*.

The story in the *Daily Express* was called *From Benefit Mum to Property Millionaire,* and that is one way to describe my life. My marriage split up when my children were very young — they were only eighteen months and three years old — and I ended up moving into the back bedroom of my parents' house. From there, I decided to go and get a university degree because I hadn't really excelled at school. I think I was about twenty-eight when I went to university, and obviously I was a mature student and a mum. I absolutely adored the learning and thrived in the environment, and from there I ended up as a university lecturer.

I did that for the next eleven years on a part-time basis. But then the worse thing happened, and I ended up being made redundant from a job I adored. Within three or four months of being made redundant, I got an invitation to what turned out to be a long weekend of personal development. This took me on a journey into understanding what goals were, understanding leverage and action learning, which, considering I was a university lecturer, was a bit odd that I hadn't come across any of this stuff before. It was also my first introduction to a book called, *Rich Dad Poor Dad.*
I already had my own home and a property at the time, but I would not have called myself in any shape or form a "property investor." My intention was to be a coach, and I knew nothing about the property market.

It's funny how the universe intervenes, and soon after finishing a year of personal development, I started to get letters inviting me to a talk on property investment. By February 2008, I was on a three-day training course and ended up signing up for £20,000 worth of training. My partner Bob, my sister, my brother-in-law and I, put together some money for a house and so our journey began. By June, I had my first offer on a property accepted and by August we had completed. It was hell, but it still remains one of the better properties in the portfolio.

I'd learned a lot about the buying process, BMV (Below Market Value) properties, mortgage fraud and all that stuff. Then suddenly, things got really difficult — it wasn't anything like it had been taught in the class, and it wasn't easy. Property investing was a real challenge. More offers were falling through than were being accepted. I was wasting money on surveys and brokers, and I decided something had to change. I worked on my goals and mindset again.

The change was amazing; literally from 2009 onwards, I was buying on average one to two properties per month. I already had a system and a model, but then I learned where I was making the mistakes. I made some changes and improvements, and that's how I am where I am now.

So property investing wasn't like it was taught in the class. And this is why you started writing books?

Yes, I think that was the driver. As I got towards the end of 2009, I found lots of people were saying to me, "It's alright for you, you have money," which was a huge assumption. Each of us had put £20,000 in the pot: we had £80,000 pounds to invest, which was peanuts. I mean it's a lot of money in the grand scheme of things, but in property investing terms it was not a lot compared to what some people were investing. Our strategy was never to do with the volume of money — it was trying to find the best way to make that money work for us.

I had a coach who was encouraging me to do a collaborative project so that I could learn to outsource rather than doing everything myself. I smile when I say this because the idea was to have twelve friends coming together and write two or three pages each, then my role was to get someone else to design a cover. But instead, it turned into this 60,000-word book written by me. That particular book *Using Other People's Money: How to Invest in Property* has now been completely re-written three times under the same title. The latest edition was published in September 2014, and I've written two more books since then. For me, writing books is about wanting to share with people my experience of property, I'm quite happy to write down the good, the bad and the ugly of what's happened and if others learn from my mistakes and build on my successes, that's really all I want.

Tell me more about your books and how they all differ from each other.

Well, there are three books. The first book, as I mentioned, I have now written three times mainly because things change so much in the property market that it wasn't a case of just a quick edit. I really wanted to give my latest thoughts, experience and opinions on each strategy. The book is called *Using Other People's Money — How to Invest in Property.* I look at each of the strategies that have been used in the past, and that are currently being used now, and I explain particularly how they worked for me. In other words, what worked well, what didn't work, and how they will work for the reader in terms of how much time and money they'll take. This is so the readers can understand, given any circumstance that they are in, which is the best strategy for them.

It is easy to go to a property event and one person in the room — maybe the speaker — will be passionate about their strategy, and everybody in the room will think, 'That's great, I'm off to do that strategy.' But what they don't understand is where that person started from, what experience they had, how much time or money they had, or what was driving them. Of course, that may not be the same for the audience member. If they were in full-time employment, then running a large rent-to-rent portfolio might not be the easiest route. But if they went into that strategy knowing that it was going to take a lot of time, it's a great place to start for somebody with very little money. Successful property investment is all about understanding what you're getting yourself into with each of the strategies.

My second book is called *Make More Money from Property: From Investor Thinking to a Business Mindset.* I wrote this book so people would stop thinking like property investors and start thinking like business owners. The secret is to recognise that what they do is a repeatable model and that they can do this for others for a fee. A lot of people I meet tell me how great they've been at investing in property, they've gone off and bought these houses and made all these brilliant contacts, but then they've run out of money. This happens to a lot of people — if you don't have a lot of money to start with, you may only be able to buy that first property. Then, they explain that they are now doing share trading or something else instead of cultivating the great model that they already had, which had been so successful for them. They've got the build team, the letting agent, the estate agent and so on. But they go and do something completely different, when they could do that for somebody else and probably make more money in fees for a fully packaged service.

The last book is more for the general public. That's called *Property For the Next Generation: Preparing Your Family for a Wealthy Future*. This book is really directed at the general public, helping to let them know why property is such a good idea. It's not the glitzy glamour stuff of television shows like *Homes Under the Hammer* — which teaches you that you can buy a wreck at auction, spend a couple of thousand pounds and it will be worth a million! Instead, it's about recognising that we are a country and a culture, bred to want to own our own home, which is fabulous but owning your home is actually owning a "liability." In contrast, owning a property portfolio is owning an income-generating "asset," which means you can choose to live wherever you want.

The children of the next generation who are growing up now — the "flicky finger" generation — they are going to have such different lives to us, our parents and our grandparents. We need to be preparing our families for this future and not basing our decisions about property investment on what our parents and grandparents thought. The world they lived in was so different from the world our children will live in, so leaving one crusty old mansion that's been in the family for generations, to be shared between two or three children may not be the best long-term wealth-creating strategy. The probate forced sale may (almost certainly) come at the wrong time for the market. This is just one of a whole lot of myths that I bust for the general public.

You've recently been named as one of the most influential people in property by *The Daily Telegraph*. That came about from your books didn't it?

Yes, it did. I think the most important thing that books give you is a level of credibility, especially if it's a good book and people read it. I must say that I did use PR, so I made sure that I wrote articles around the subjects of my books. I wasn't just taking chapters out of the books and repurposing them. I was taking my material and reworking it so that my writing was appropriate to the journal or magazine that I wanted to be published in. Some of those pieces were more opinionated than they were in the book, and some of those pieces were fact and tip based.

I appeared on the radar of *The Telegraph* at just the right time. They were launching their Property Club, and I was invited to be in the first piece and was interviewed by the journalist. It was me, Phil Spencer (presenter of Channel 4's *Location, Location, Location*) and some other bloke. Then they kept referring to me as Wusche and sent a photographer to spend ninety minutes taking one photo that was so small you could not see the background anyway! Now, the journalist gets in touch every couple of months and asks me to contribute to a piece he's doing, or he'll pick up on a piece I've sent out and shape that to his purpose. Then I got the news that I was listed in the top twenty-five most influential people in property; what a great privilege and quite a giggle too.

Every author has a different writing process — so tell me more about yours. Do you wake up one morning and have an idea and write around it? How do you structure your writing time?

I get a lot of my ideas in the shower. Often, in the morning when I'm just standing there, and the water is pounding on my head, there must be something about that connection that washes out an idea. If it's good enough, I grab it and hold onto it until I get to the office. Then I usually percolate or cultivate the idea for a little while. It's alright having an idea, but it's developing it into something people want to read that's the bigger challenge. That process can take anything from a couple of weeks to a couple of months; it depends on how the idea came to me in the first place and how clear it was when it came to me.

When I write, I write very specifically for someone. I have their name and their face in my head when I write. I think when you can define who your audience is in a clear way, then people will pick up your book and read it and say, "It's like you're writing to *me.*" It's also about the cover, the title, the images, the words on the back of the book. They must all speak to that one person that you've been writing to all the way along — so they will love the book and get the most out of it. If other people pick it up and put it down because they don't think it's for them, that's great as they were never going to get your message and were never going to take the action that you want them to take as a result of reading the book. So that's the creative process.

I've tried writing in two different ways actually. With my first three books — *Other People's Money, Make More Money* and *Property for the Next Generation,* I just sat and wrote them. I felt that having a structure would slow down the process of writing. It felt like I was taking dictation from myself, I knew what I wanted to say, so I just wrote it.

The fourth title I'm writing at the moment is called *The Business of Investment,* and I have written in a very different way. I wanted to pitch it to publishers, so I wrote descriptions of what would be in the chapters before writing the book. I feel it has really caused my writing style to slow down because instead of just getting on and writing what I want to write about, I have to do what I said I would write in the next chapter. So this has felt a bit odd, almost a bit constraining. When I speak at events, I tend to be unscripted, and that was how I wrote until now. But if I want the attention of the publishers I have to follow their templates.

So you've felt restricted by having to agree on a book structure with a publisher beforehand.

Yes, very much constricted by it, though the silly thing is the content will still be the same; it's just been my speed of writing.

Personally, I don't implement a writing regime of getting up for two hours in the morning and writing. I find that start-stop technique doesn't help my creativity. If I am in the flow, if I'm in the mood, I will just write all day. If I am planning to write, I usually mark two weeks out on my diary. Each of the first five versions of the books I wrote took me between five and seven working days over a two-week period to just get it down on paper. The idea of dragging it out for years and months seems mad — how will the information still be relevant two years later when the book is finally published?

Where is your favourite place to write your books?

I have an office at home, and I have staff in the office, but they are quite quiet. If I want to be really quiet, then I move a desk into my bedroom, and I will sit up there and get away from the phone. I will not have the Internet on. When I am writing, if I know there are some statistics I need, I just change to red font and say what it is I want to find, then I'll do that research afterwards. I don't go backwards and forwards. I just write and write: no Internet, no phone, and the words come out very easily then, uninterrupted.

Tell me about your book launches and what you do for them.

I didn't do anything for the very first book. I didn't know how many books to order or anything. I ordered five hundred books from the printer, and they were delivered. I lined them up in my front room, and I sat there that evening saying to Bob, my partner, "Oh look, the books have arrived." He said, "Oh great, what are you doing with them?" and I thought, 'I have no idea. I've written it, I've got it published, and I suppose now I have to sell it.' I didn't know how to sell a book, I didn't know how to get it on Amazon, and I had no idea about any kind of marketing.

By the time I published my second book, *Make More Money from Property,* we had an official book launch. I hired a small private restaurant that would close down for the night and just have us there. I sold tickets and gave people dinner, wine, and a copy of the book. The third book I launched at The Business Show. I'd spoken a few times there and given keynote talks, so I asked them if I could have one of their side rooms and then advertise that I was doing my book launch there, so people came along to that. Very different approaches.

I know what people say about having a launch, but I think the party can be more stress because you are thinking, 'Who's going to come?' at a time when you should be focused on selling your book. A book launch is really for you to celebrate with your friends — do something else that's more fun and less stress.

I think what you do need with a book launch is a "Ta-daaa!" date. This is the date your book's going to be released — your publishing date — and you must let people know about it. Letting half a dozen people know so they can come and get a free glass of wine is less important than making sure it's on Amazon, and that you've been tweeting and Facebooking about it in advance. Hopefully, if you do it right, you end up having a social media "following" or "tribe" even before the book is printed, so by the time the book comes out, people are desperate to buy a copy.

Do you prefer online or offline marketing ahead of your book launch?

I think if I were to do it in the right order, I would still have my cake and eat it. Having said that, I don't think a party is a good idea, I would still want a party! However, I'd make sure that I had a good following online first: I'd be speaking about my book at events, I'd be mentioning it on my website, on Facebook and Twitter and everything else. So, by the time I knew that my book was going to be launched, I'd already have people liking it and following the page. Then, I could still have a party and know that plenty of people would want to come, and I'd be over-subscribed. But the party would be the cherry on the icing on the cake because the main marketing and promotion work would have been done. The message that there is a book out there that's coming is more important than just a party and a glass of wine.

Your cover design and book title are very important aren't they — especially when it comes to sales and promotion?

They are very important. I spend a lot of time talking about the book title — checking on search engines and making sure that no one else has got that title. I think about the website, about a Twitter handle for it and all that sort of stuff, then work with a good designer. There is always the temptation to get a cheap book cover done from somewhere like 99 Designs or do it yourself with stock pictures you find online. But I think if you are going to make writing a central part of your business process, then you need a bespoke stand-out image or a cover that adds value to your words and says something to a different group of people. So yes, I think that's really important.

Have your books helped you get more speaking engagements?

Yes, definitely. I'm not sure if I would have got speaking gigs without the books in the early days. There are very few girls in property — you could mention them on one hand — but how many of them get speaking gigs? We're not often seen on the big stage.

Certainly, when you look at the Business Show, the dominant keynote speakers are male. I wouldn't have got keynote slots at the Business Show if it weren't for the books, and I certainly wouldn't have been in the newspapers.

Why aren't I out there just buying houses? Because I have reached the stage where I don't want any more properties, I am just looking to churn what I've got. I'm not looking to have two hundred and fifty properties. Sometimes when you speak to the boys, they are all into how many properties they've got. I would rather have fewer properties that give me the right amount of income and just the right amount of time so I can have the lifestyle that I want. I'm not one for flashy watches, pointy shoes, a helicopter or a fast car.

Once you get enough income from property, you start to re-evaluate how you want to spend your time. I love buying houses but don't want to manage the tenants (and they are where the cash flow comes from!). So I satisfy my need to shop by sourcing properties for bespoke clients. On top of that, I think I am a teacher at heart. I love sharing what I have learned and helping others to achieve their goals, so that is why I also have The Sourcer's Apprentice — my training business.

What have been the high points and the low points of writing your books?

I think the biggest challenge is that when you're in book writing mode, you're not selling, and you're in a different headspace. A book doesn't make you money unless you have "*Grey*" in the title — I might have to write *50 Grey Shades of Property!* You make money or create a business through normal business-based books by charging for a product or service that you get your client to buy after they've read your book. Business books are a marketing tool. Yes, I make income from my books, obviously, but it's not my primary work.

I think the highlight for me was when my father picked up my first book and told me how proud he was of me — that was a high point. They still lay my books out on the dining room table so visitors can see them! My father is a strict Italian, and I experienced an English education that always left me feeling like maybe I was never as clever as he is because he is a very clever man. I didn't write the book to make my father proud, but that was a big bonus!

Another thing is the testimonials you get from complete strangers. I met someone at a speaking gig last week, and they said, "I've printed out your diagram from your book, and I have it on my wall to remind me." Some of the concepts I have developed and written about in my books, especially about understanding how you use your time, are not expressed in that way by anybody else I've read. These new ways of expressing old ideas help my readers to think differently about how they run their business or their lives. So knowing that I have just shared something that is helping someone else to do what they want in their life is just an awesome thing, particularly when they are strangers. Writing a book is almost like giving a gift without any concern about getting a thank you — then not knowing how many people have taken you up on the gift. When someone does come back and say, "I read your book last year and it made this difference for me" or "I've got a bit of your book printed on my wall, and it makes this difference for me," it is just superb. It's like the best Christmas present ever.

You are known as The Property Mermaid. Tell me how that branding came about and how it ties in with your books?

A friend of mine, Thomas Power, who founded Ecademy, with his wife Penny Power OBE, is an incredible networker. He used to arrange opportunities to meet up with people and get to know them better. I think as a way of remembering everybody, he would group things about them such as their interests, their name and what they did. Then, he would pull them altogether so that he could then say, for example, "You're Stephanie Hale, the book lady."

We were talking about why I got into property, and I said, "It's because I always felt I was the undiscovered granddaughter of Jacques Cousteau: all I ever wanted to do was scuba dive. When I was a university lecturer, we had great holidays, but I never wanted to create a business that meant I had to work 24/7. So I discovered a strategy and a model for me in property investing, which meant that I could have holidays whenever I wanted them." So he called me, "The Property Mermaid." That became a blog, and it is a lot easier than saying or trying to spell "Wusche," and it's just fun. Also, Vicki can be spelt differently, whereas you can put "property mermaid" in the search engines and find me and my books. It's memorable, and it just makes me much easier to find!

We haven't spoken much about property — what are you doing now?

Over the last two years, I have been focusing on developing and growing my businesses. The Property Sourcers works with bespoke clients who are looking for a net return on their cash investments. I don't do joint ventures or anything complicated. I just source property for people with money to invest and in return I earn a healthy fee.

The Sourcer's Apprentice is my training business as mentioned before, and it's under this umbrella that I write the books. I have online courses in everything from using Excel to understand the numbers in a deal, to how to source and how to set up a successful property business. Then in late 2014, I started to offer exclusive one-day events to just a dozen business owners at a time. These are great fun and really bring all my teaching skills, coaching skills and business experience together in one place. Then, of course, I coach and mentor a small number of people either one-to-one if they are serious and determined or in a group if they just need the accountability and community.

I still love speaking, and always say that any night I am out talking at an event, is a night Bob — my ever patient and loving partner — gets to sit at home in peace and quiet.

IDEAS FOR YOU

- When looking for inspiration, leave your ideas to percolate for a while to see if they're worth developing.

- Write specifically for *someone*. Have a face in your head when you write. Your reader should feel: "It's like you're writing this book for *me*."

- Write down "the good, the bad and the ugly" of your property journey and share it so other people can learn from your mistakes and build on your successes.

- Mark out two weeks in your diary to write your book. If you're in the flow, write all day!

- Remove all distractions while you're writing. Turn off the Internet and phone.

- Leave out any statistics in your first draft and research them later.

- Writing books for publishers may feel constraining as you may need to follow a "template."

- Avoid the temptation to get a cheap book cover if you are self-publishing. Use a bespoke design that adds value to your words.

- Publicise your publication date on Facebook, Twitter and other social media in advance. Build a following *before* your book is launched.

- For publicity, write articles around the subjects in your book. Rework your material so it's appropriate to the journal or magazine you want to be published in.

- If some people pick your book up and put it down because they don't think it's for them, that's great because they'd never have "got" your message.

FRANCIS DOLLEY

"From a monetary point of view, the payback was almost instant..."

Francis Dolley is one of the most sought-after property trainers in his specialist Rent-to-Rent niche, and he has spoken to thousands of property investors all over the UK.

A former builder, he started full-time property investing in 2010, along with his wife and two grown-up children. Since then he's built up a property portfolio of both owned and leased properties that have replaced his family's income several times over.

Francis is author of *Mayhem, Murder and Multi-Lets* — a warts-and-all account of his baptism of fire into property investing, right through to how he discovered a simple yet hugely effective system that enabled him and his family to become financially independent in six short months.

The inspiration for the book came after a late-night conversation I had in a bar. It was after a property meeting in Bristol. There was a group of guys who were sitting around telling stories about dodgy tenants and slippery agents.

It came to my turn, and so I was telling my stories about my formative years in property. It brought forth a lot of gasps of shock and horror along with looks of concern and roars of laughter. As we were all putting on our coats to leave, somebody said that I should write a book. I guess that's when the idea started growing. So, I'm sorry to say that, yes, the idea came from a late-night conversation in a bar.

So, share some more about the content of your book. *Mayhem, Murder & Multi-Lets* is an unusual title for a property book.

I think because there are a lot of serious property books already out there, I just thought the world didn't really need another one. I did agonise over the name as you can probably imagine. I find in life the way to approach things is to simplify things as much as you can. So, I was thinking about my life in property, and I kind of divided it into three sections. When I first got into property, I didn't have a clue what I was doing at all, and I completely took my eye off the ball. This resulted in two years of absolute mayhem where anything and everything that could possibly go wrong did go spectacularly wrong and then some. When I look back, I do wonder how I coped as I also had a very busy building company to run (which probably explains it!).

We had put all that drama behind us and settled into a fairly uneventful property life. Then a couple years ago, one of our tenants murdered his step-mum in the street in the middle of the afternoon in Bristol. That was a kind of defining moment for us I guess in our property life, where we thought, 'We REALLY need to get things totally under control' (not that we could have done much about this particular situation). By this time, we had also started investing in multi-lets, which is renting houses room by room to maximise the potential profits.

When I was thinking about it, it suddenly hit me that all these three sections in my life began with an M, and it just seemed to flow well: *Mayhem, Murder & Multi-Lets*. So, I guess it was like the three Ms of property. Also, I was very aware that you need great headlines to grab a reader's attention, as they do in newspapers. I wanted my title to read like a headline. I wanted it to have a little bit of intrigue I guess, for people to think, 'Is it a property book or is it a fiction book?'

Tell me about the design on the front cover. A lot of people have images on the front cover, but you've gone for more of an attention-grabbing headline instead.

Well, part of my research was that I looked on Amazon, and I was scanning through all the books. For me, if there's a book with a picture of the author on the front of it, it was hard for me to determine what the book was about without reading the entire blurb, and not everyone's got time to do that. What I decided I needed was an attention-grabbing headline that would instantly give you a feel for the book.

The ones where it actually had the name on the book, it leapt right out at me. I envisaged then that my books would be on shelves some day in the future. If there's something on the front of a book that's going to grab people straight off, then I thought, 'there's more chance they're going to buy my book,' because in reality in today's fast-paced world you've only got a few seconds to hold their attention.

Tell me how long it took between having that conversation in the bar and you getting cracking on it?

I think it's fair to say that most people have this kind of idea that they'd like to write a book — at some time in the future! I think from that conversation I had in the bar that evening in Bristol, until the day I went onto a property course — it was a brilliant course by a lady called Stephanie Hale. Do you know her? [Laughs]. That took me about six months I would say. In fact, even then, it was my wife Jane who booked me on as a birthday present and if not for her I may well still be on the starting blocks.

Then I reckon there were eighteen months of procrastinating when I was telling myself I would get around to it someday. I was just doing kind of half an hour here and half an hour there on it. So, in all, I probably put it off for a good two years.

And did you make any worthwhile notes or write any chapters during those two years?

I think I had the initial names of the chapters (these changed as the book evolved) and a skeleton outline of each one, but it was in very rough form. In fact, I started a completely different book and got further with that one before I returned my attention back to MMM! The other book will be out in the spring — once you have the writing bug you just can't stop. I guess I write a book like a painter would create a canvas. First the outline, then some colourful in-fill, and finally the detail.

So, what were the challenges along the way that blocked

you finishing it?

Funny you should ask that! For me, it was life — because we run a really busy property training business, as well as renting the actual properties, and both these companies were new and rapidly expanding. So, there were all the usual challenges along the way, plus I've got a family and a busy social life.

But most of all, I think the thing that held me back from beginning and then finishing the book were the constant distractions. People call this "the age of information," but I think when people look back on it, it will become known as "the age of constant distractions," with constant real-time social media interruptions and a veritable avalanche of e-mails to deal with each and every day. So, it was only really when I learned to switch it all off and ignore it that I was able to focus a good amount of time on writing the actual book. It was a revelation for me to realize that I was far more efficient if I grouped my tasks and focused my time on individual subjects, rather than trying to constantly multi-task. This vastly increased my productivity and freed up hours of additional time that I could then spend on MMM without feeling that I was neglecting my property business.

Explain how you got it finished ...

I've got a good friend who was going to stay in Florida for three months, and he asked me if I wanted to come over for ten days. I thought it would be a great opportunity for me to get away from everything and everybody and be able to focus on my book. So I jumped at the chance.

One of the things I did was to leave my mobile phone at home. Pause for effect! To be perfectly honest, I didn't mean to leave my phone at home, I forgot it. I only realized when I was halfway to the airport. But in actual fact, it was the best thing that could have happened. By the time I got over the angst of not having my phone on me at all times, I sent my son an e-mail saying, "If there's anything urgent that happens at home, would you call me or send me an e-mail?"

During the ten days I was in America, he never called or e-mailed me at all. So, having to be in constant contact with the world I think is a fallacy of the age. Not having my phone and not having all the distractions helped me exponentially — so much in fact that I got about half the book done. But that may explain why there are some Americanisms and spellings in the book, I guess!

So the lack of distractions was a huge factor in me finishing the book — and the fact that I had set myself a deadline to get it finished

So, the time factor as much as anything.

Yes, because when I didn't have anything to aim for, then it was all a bit woolly. But as soon as I had a firm date to aim for, then I could implement a plan of action and put things in place to make sure I had enough time to get it done. I think it's true to say that everyone works better to a deadline. Set yourself a target, and you have something to aim at. I knew what date I wanted the finished book in my hand. I knew how long the editing and creation process was, so then I knew how many days I had to get my part (the writing) done. I knew roughly how many words I wanted and, therefore, how many words I needed to write each and every day. I'm not saying I hit my target every day, but it was a good framework.

What were your feelings prior to the actual launch of your book? Were you nervous?

Not really. I'm the sort of person that if I decide to go for it, it's full steam ahead and damn the torpedoes! I'm very visual as well. So, what I would do is to run a scenario through my head over and over. I was going to the book launch, and I was going to speak at the event. The books were all there, and everyone in the audience had one held up in the air with a big smile on their faces. People were happy and were clapping. I just ran the whole thing through my head endlessly, so that when the day arrived it felt a bit like déjà vu. Is this normal or am I weird? It works for me — it's kinda like *The Secret* [by Rhonda Byrne]: clearly and precisely ask the Universe for what you want, and the Universe will grant your wish!

So I just knew the book launch was going to go well. But also I think that having a good team of people around you is crucial. I now have a great little team of people who work in the property business and at the events that we run, and they were all there on the night. Everybody had a role to play, so we all knew exactly what we had to do, and it was like a super-slick machine (with one of two mini-panics thrown in for prosperity)!

You had a really fun campaign on social media in the run-up to your launch. Tell me about some of the things that you did.

I think the last thing people want is for any budding author to be just rapping on about their own books. So I searched out lots of images and pictures on the Internet of astronauts in space; pictures of the Queen; a picture of an airplane pulling a banner behind it; poster adverts at bus stops; famous guys; in fact, all sorts of interesting and unusual pictures from anywhere. Then I inserted an image of my book into the pictures. There was my book in the hands lots of famous people! A lot of people said the one that was the most hilarious was the picture of the Queen reading my book, but I really loved the guy in the gorilla suit holding a placard with the MMM book on it. I did it to create a buzz and to get people talking about MMM and get them interested and intrigued.

You had Oprah as well, didn't you?

Oh yes, of course, how could I forget Oprah? She was on her show, and there was my book — she seemed to be enjoying it. My book was appearing on people's desks, on their shelves, it was just appearing everywhere. We played a game in the office every day for a week to see who could think up the best 'positioning' of the book. We even snuck a few onto a shelf at WH Smith's and took a photo. We left one behind for some lucky person!

Sometimes it was like a game of *Where's Wally?* where you have to search out the book — it was always in the pictures some place. Because social media is so big, and everything is interconnected like an enormous spider's web, I would tag some friends and colleagues into the pictures, as well. Then, of course, that image would go on their pages. Then it was seen by their friends, and the MMM virus spread really fast. The power of social media is frighteningly huge.

You had a fantastic launch at the UK's largest property network meeting. Tell me about that and all the planning that went into it.

Yes, I had unexpectedly been asked to speak at this prestigious event, and so this was the rock solid date I'd set to have the book finished and actually in my hands. I wanted to make the talk a lot of fun to reflect the book, with lots of insights and a few ahhhh moments. Some property events talks can be very factual and very dry. Whereas I believe that as well as informing or educating an audience, you should also entertain. People have left the comfort of their own home and even their family to come and listen to you, so you should at least make sure they have a good time!

So, my talk was actually named *Mayhem, Murder & Multi-Lets*, the same as my book. As I said, I wanted it to include a lot of very useful information that people could implement in their property businesses, a lot of golden nuggets and most of all, at some point in the evening I wanted to surprise people with a gift of my book — because I think most people like a good surprise!

The event was sold out — there were two hundred and thirty people and more chairs had to be gathered from the next room to accommodate them. I got there mid-afternoon with my team, and we taped a book underneath each and every chair, which of course took some time. We had to experiment to get the right sort of tape, and then we were sitting down hard on the chairs and standing up to make sure the books weren't going to fall onto the floor. So, there were a lot of really technical logistics going on in the background.

At this event, the usual way things go is that there's a draw, and one person gets a book or a DVD set. But I wanted everybody in the room to have a book so nobody would go home feeling disappointed. It was a brilliant moment when everybody in the room realized that they had got a prize — just for being there in the first place. It was all about logistics and organisation, and the evening went like a military campaign.

There were also some really fun photos all over Facebook afterwards.

Yes, I did prime the photographer. I said, "There will be times when I need you to take a specific picture." Once everyone had pulled a book out from under their chair, I said, "Stand and hold the books up in the air as high as you can," which they very kindly did. As everyone was so happy to receive an unexpected gift, they were smiling from ear to ear, and it made a brilliant photo. There was a line in the book that read, *and that person is you.* I highlighted it in one book and placed the book randomly in the audience. The person who had the lucky book won a place on a forthcoming event. This, again was a bundle of fun and another great photo.

Then, I played a little trick on people. I asked half the audience to stand up with their hands shoulder width apart, and other people to stand up with their hands together, and we took a picture of that. Of course, when you see the photograph it looks like I'm getting a standing ovation. So I was putting all these kind of fun elements into the evening. I think everybody said it was quite a memorable evening and very different from the normal evenings they usually have there.

What sort of feedback have you been getting generally about your book?

Phenomenal I would say. The launch of the book at the Berkshire Property Meet was quite unique. So, the book brought forth a lot of smiles and a big following I would say from that event on its own. We've got a mantra in our business that we like to over-deliver on our promises, and this was a perfect example. It's just a great feeling to give things and additionally spread a little bit of joy into the world. Everybody said what a memorable night it was, and there was real buzz in the room for the whole evening that carried on into the wee small hours when we all eventually collapsed into bed exhausted after all that networking.

What sort of value has your book added to your business?

From a monetary point of view, the payback was almost instant because at the end of the event we were giving people the opportunity to attend our forthcoming event at a special one-off low price. I think from that evening, there were about thirty or so people signed onto our event.

If most people are like me, they will have a small stack of books all lined up ready to read; they have them in their book queue. So, as people read the book over the year, more people are going to start to trickle through and onto our events. Books are like a snapshot of the author. I think people need to get to know you a bit first before they decide to do some more business with you. Having a book that's quite personal — because there are quite a lot of things in the book that are quite personal about me — people really get to know you and hopefully, to like and trust you.

Would you say it's changed people's perceptions of you?

Writing a book that covers aspects of my personal life was a little scary at times — was I really going to tell the world this stuff? Putting it all out there can also open you up to criticism, especially if you frequent social media platforms. People that organise events are sometimes referred to in a

133

derogatory way as property gurus. I dislike that phrase because the truth of it is that I just found a property niche that worked very well, and I've tried to help some other people to do the same thing. It's as simple as that really.

We're trying to build a community, so I think people have got to know me a lot more that way, as well. The e-mails I receive from people are a lot more personal than they once were like they are speaking to an old friend, and I like it that way.

Writing a book also makes you the known authority on your subject matter. In fact, you probably become more of an expert by default, as you have agonised and internalised each and every word of your book!

What sort of advice, if any, do you have for any other property experts who are thinking of writing a book?

I'd say with hindsight that I would've started a journal a long time ago. It would have made remembering all the crazy stuff a lot easier if I had recorded it all as it happened. So if you're thinking about writing a book, I think it's a good idea to start a journal right now. Aim to be writing a little bit every day, and you will soon become prolific.

I think it's a good idea to brainstorm a title even if it's a working title for now, and even chapter names. This way I found it was easier to build myself a framework and then start to fill it in. Also, you've got to know who your audience is because when I began to write my book I was really writing it for myself and this was a big mistake. Then I had some crucial advice from my brilliant mentor [Laughs]. You said, "The book is not actually for you at all, you're writing it for your audience. You've got to think who your audience is, so you should be really clear who you're going to write the book for, as well." This realization made me go back and rewrite some sections and gave me great clarity.

I think it helps to write for a set period every day. When I had a deadline, I knew how many words I needed to write every day. So I could backtrack to where I was, and then I knew exactly how much time I had to put aside each day to get the book complete. Definitely set yourself a solid deadline that you've got something to aim for — I can't emphasise how important this is.

Somebody once said to me that writing a book is the closest that a man can ever come to having a baby. I sincerely hope I never find out for sure, but I can certainly say that after all that hard work, the labour pains and the angst, it just feels really good to see it out there in the world. Just do it!

IDEAS FOR YOU

- You need an attention-grabbing book title — similar to a newspaper headline — to entice people to buy your book.

- Know who your audience is. Writing the book for yourself, rather than your reader, is a big mistake.

- Create the outline of your book first. Prepare the names of your chapters and a skeleton outline for each one. You can fill in the detail later.

- Set yourself a deadline to get your book finished. Work out how long you want your book to be and how many words you need to write each day.

- Have a team of people to help with your book launch.

- Search out unusual images and funny pictures to create a buzz for your book on social media that will quickly go viral. Create intrigue and have fun.

- People love a surprise. Consider giving away copies of your book at your launch.

- Think of other fun bonuses at your launch — such as a free ticket to one of your events — to make it really memorable.

- Offer one-off low price tickets to a forthcoming event at your launch.

- Build a friendly community around your book — treat your readers like old friends.

- Over-deliver on your promises to ensure that you have a book launch that's remembered for a long time to come.

GILL ALTON

"I've probably doubled, if not tripled speaking engagements compared with before I had the book."

Gill Alton is author of *Your Pension Shortfall, Your Retirement Rescue Plan* and has eighteen years' experience of property investment. She is the founder of hands-free property investment business, Alton Property Partners, and mentoring business, Alton Property Mentoring.

She has a personal portfolio of nineteen houses and has purchased and refurbished twenty-two houses for clients. Gill is passionate about educating those who are heading, through no fault of their own, towards a retirement marred by financial misery.

I never set out to write a book! I started writing a report for my website, but it got bigger and bigger because I'm so passionate about my subject. I found that the more research I did, the more it evolved. My inspiration was to help people understand what is happening within the pension marketplace, and how property investment has the ability to help resolve a pension shortfall.

Writing a book was one of the things on my bucket list, and I knew I always wanted it to be a book that would help people, but as I have just explained that wasn't my intention at the outset. It's just once I got into the subject, I realized that there was just too much information to cover in a short report. I felt a report would not have done it justice.

There's a lot of passion in your book, but there are also a lot of facts and statistics. How did you go about collecting all these?

It took ages to get all the facts and statistics together because I was teaching myself, and I didn't want to just write a book off the top of my head saying: "You need to invest in property to fill the pension gap". I wanted to *prove* why there was a pension gap, and I wanted to *prove* how you could use property to resolve it. I come from a family of accountants and engineers, so people who are very factual. So I decided to put myself in their shoes and asked myself, "What would they do if somebody just came along and said, 'Invest in property'?" As they're overly cautious, would they do it without the cold hard facts of reality? Knowing my family — probably not!

So, it was important for me that I wrote the book to help those who are of a more cautious nature and are new to property investing. I wanted them to be able to say, "Now I understand why I need to do it and how I do it." I pulled on my own knowledge and experience of property, but also I researched the pension market for months and months, I read lots of reports, lots of articles and spoke to Independent Financial Advisers.

I'm fortunate I was able to work with the help of my mum, a retired accountant. She checked all my spreadsheets — and there were a lot of them — as I compared pension results to property investment results.

In fact, there were over three hundred spreadsheet pages of analysis before they were whittled down to about forty, which were used to share the story in my book. To be honest, the analysis took a tremendous amount of time because things were constantly changing in the pensions' world, or I found I had omitted something important. If I had done more planning up front, I probably could have saved considerable time writing my book, and the re-work would certainly have been less. A lesson learnt the hard way!

So it's a huge body of research, as much as it is a book?

Yes, that's a good way of looking at it. However, having brought all this research together, it was important to me to write my book in a way that people understood it. That's why I introduced a character throughout called David, because I wanted people to have someone they could associate with and think, 'Oh, that's like me.' Without David, I was concerned it would just be a big volume of research that would be too heavy going. Particularly as I know if you say the word "pension" to most people they go, "Ugh" or glaze over. But the truth is a lot of the problems being faced today are because people have paid little or no interest in their pension; they think they will 'sort it out' in the future. Unfortunately, the future has a habit of sneaking up on us, so I knew I had to do it in a way that got the story across and brought important information in front of people.

You went through a dozen or more titles for your book, didn't you? Tell me about some of your titles and why you rejected them.

I can't remember all the titles I rejected [Laughs]. I tried to come up with wacky titles and catchy titles, but they didn't work. Then I thought, 'I need to go back to what's actually in the story; what's it telling people.' I settled on *Your Pension Shortfall, Your Retirement Rescue Plan as the* word "pension" is highly searched in Google, as is "retirement." I decided to look at it from the point of view of what keyword searches my readers might make.

Also, as the book was very factual, I thought it deserved a powerful, factual title, rather than some sort of wisecrack title.

Again, with the book cover, I remember there were a number of different images. I think they included a golden egg, a tree and a life jacket?

Designing the cover followed a similar process to choosing the title. As you know, I looked at quite a few images. Every time I changed the title, I changed the image. So once I ruled out those titles, the images also had to go. I decided the image needed to be more hard-hitting, more straightforward.

Also, while attending your course, you had mentioned that when viewing a book on Amazon you only see a thumbnail of the cover. So, I was very conscious that I wanted the text to stand out even at the reduced size. I did several mock-ups. Other people suggested I put my photo on the front. To be honest, I did struggle with that one for a long time because I'm not really the sort of person to put my photo on everything. But once I saw it, and we got the colours for the text and background right, I was very happy. I felt it looked both professional and personal, which was my aim.

You could have gone for a straightforward 5 x 9 book cover, but you didn't. Explain why you chose bigger dimensions.

I went for a bigger size because there are so many tables and diagrams in my book. I've read standard-sized books where they have tables and charts, and I've struggled to read them even with my glasses on — so I wanted my book to be different.

I thought about my target market, people in their mid-forties upwards. If they are like me, then their eyesight is probably getting slightly less clear with age, so I wanted to make it easy for them. I didn't want to instantly turn people off because they couldn't read half the diagrams.

I know you agonised for a while about the pricing of your book. How did you finally decide on your price?

I knew the content value of the book was worth well over £20, but I felt that £20 was a watershed; I thought that some people would think it was too much if it was above this. So I chose £19.99 to be just below the £20 watershed.

Which books have sold better for you, e-books or paperbacks?

I haven't converted my book into an e-book or Kindle

book, simply because there are so many diagrams within it. I felt there was no point in getting a Kindle version created if readers couldn't see the images. I know you can drag images out to make them bigger, but there's something like seventy images in my book, and I thought having to keep stopping and make images bigger would be an annoyance to the reader. It could dilute the important messages I am trying to get across in the book.

You've used quite a few charts and graphs from other sources. How easy was it to get permission to use these?

There are about five or six. I wrote for permission and then used their data and had the charts re-designed by your team. Each asked to see the finished chart to check they were happy with it, and they wanted me to reference their source. In each case, thankfully they were happy with what we produced. So, actually this process was a lot easier than I thought it was going to be, and I believe you were even surprised with the ease we moved through this stage. There were no charges or fees to be paid.

Tell me about the sort of things you have done to promote your book. I know you run Facebook ads, and it's been on sale at property meets …

It's mostly been through social media and networking, and obviously it's on Amazon. I also promote it on Twitter, highlighting points taken from it, with a link. Many of my biggest sales to date have been at property meets and through my husband's mortgage business, Alton Mortgages Ltd.

As I've said, my book talks to people who *aren't* investing today to say, "You need to have a Retirement Plan B," you can't just rely on your traditional pension. But it was also important to me to remind those who *are* investing today to make sure that their Plan B actually delivers against their goals. So, for example, in the book there's a section where I cover in detail the *interest-only* versus *repayment* mortgage debate, from a retirement viewpoint. The fact is it's very different if you start investing in property when you're in your twenties or thirties, than if you start at mid-forties or fifties, as your timeline is much shorter to secure a retirement income in your pocket.

Often, when I'm presenting, I'll have existing investors say to me afterwards, "I didn't realize that. I need to go back and look at my portfolio."

Does being an author change the way you're perceived? Has writing a book altered the way people think of you?

Yes, I believe so. I think it's helped position me as a person who understands the nuts and bolts of pensions, and this coupled with my existing property knowledge is a powerful combination. As most people have very limited understanding of pensions, it has helped evaluate and reposition me as someone to talk to. I have people say, "Give Gill a call because she'll know the answer to that."

How would you say your business and personal branding was before your book, compared with your branding since?

They're very different. My old branding was focused on, "I'm a mum with young children — if I can do it, you can do it." With the book, I consciously wanted to reposition myself to say, "I've been in the property business for eighteen years, and I'm knowledgeable about this. This is a big issue you need to know about." So my brand and website needed to be more professional in its approach.

My website was rebranded in line with how the book looked, so it was much more professional. I also decided to take the bold step of putting my photo on my business card; I used the same image that's on my book for continuity.

What sort of feedback have you received from people who've read your book?

I've been delighted with how it's been received. It has sixteen reviews on Amazon — fourteen of which are five stars! So I really couldn't have asked for better because I know people don't write reviews freely. I have also had people phone me and say, "I've read your book, and it's really making me think differently," and I've met numerous people at property meetings who've told me, "I've never heard someone say it that way before, now I understand it."

Excellent. Has it opened up any extra speaking opportunities or business partnerships for you?

Yes, it has. I've had a lot more speaking opportunities because of it. I've probably doubled if not tripled speaking engagements over the course of this year compared with before I had the book. It's also opened up doors for me to engage with another company on a joint venture basis, which is exciting.

I chose to write about something that I'm extremely passionate about and because of that I believe it has opened up more opportunities because I am authentic and speak from the heart.

Many authors feel nervous right before a book comes out. What were your emotions immediately before your launch?

Huge relief, actually that I was finally there! Yes, I was nervous; after all, your book is your baby that you have nurtured. As you know, it took me twelve months of really hard work because of all the background research.

Letting go of a baby that you have cared for and struggled over and showing it to the world was both exciting and nerve-racking all rolled into one. I remember when the first proof of the book came through with the cover on, I danced around the house because it was suddenly real. But I must confess when it was first printed I remember thinking, "Now everybody's got a chance to read it. What if people don't understand where I'm coming from?" You do feel quite exposed at that point. That is until you get a surge of people coming back and giving you positive feedback.

What have been your main challenges throughout the entire process of writing, publishing and promoting your book?

Low points: how many times I had to change my spreadsheets. It was either that I'd made an error, or something had to be changed that impacted all three hundred spreadsheet pages. This was particularly so because, as you know, the book evolved as opposed to me planning it right from the start. I would say that was my biggest learning curve. If and when I write a second book, it will be planned to the nth degree, so that it's easier to fill the gaps in, which is, of course, what you taught when I came on your course.

Also, I had to teach myself to write succinctly. I have a newfound respect for writers, as I had many rework versions.

What kept me going was the thought, 'If I don't do it,

nobody else is going to. This story needs to be told and, therefore, I need to keep going.'

Often, authors are slightly nervous about approaching other people to ask them for testimonials. How did you feel about that?

Yes, I was nervous and, to be honest, I doubted myself at that stage. If I wrote another book, however, I would feel more confident seeking these. This would certainly be something I would change next time.

You mentioned writing another book. Would you self-publish next time or would you prefer a mainstream publisher?

No, I'd definitely self-publish. After all the joy of self-publishing is that you can just do it. You haven't got to jump through loads of hoops, so technically you are able to get it out there quickly, even if I took my time [laughs].

148

IDEAS FOR YOU

- Put yourself in your readers' shoes. Ask yourself what they'd do if somebody came along and told them: "Invest in property." What can you do to reassure them?

- Research your facts thoroughly. Read reports, articles, and speak to independent financial advisers.

- Plan your book out *before* you start rather than letting it evolve while writing it, to save yourself time on redrafting.

- Create a fictional character to bring facts to life as this will give your reader someone they can relate to. Too many facts and figures can be off-putting to readers.

- Try lots of book titles — wacky titles, catchy titles and titles with keywords your readers are searching for — before you find one you're happy with.

- Your book title should stand out, even when it's viewed at a reduced size on Amazon.

- If you use a lot of tables and diagrams in your book, these may not display well in a standard 5 x 9 format, so consider a larger size book. Make it easy for people to read your diagrams.

- Apply for permission if you are using other people's data. Get charts and graphs re-designed so that they look different from the originals.

- Use property meets to sell and promote your book.

- Update your website and business cards in line with how the book looks.

- Self-publish — you don't have to jump through so many hoops and you get the book out much faster.

IAIN WALLIS

"It was like the first day of the Harrods sale; it went absolutely crazy with people trying to get hold of the book!"

Iain Wallis is a full-time property investor and a tax strategist with over thirty years' experience.

He's featured in the popular BBC television programme 'Under the Hammer' where experts uncover the tricks of the property auction trade.

Despite the worst recession seen in the UK, he has taken his portfolio to £3.3 million since 2006.

He's author of *Legally Avoid Property Taxes: 51 Top Tips to Save Property Taxes and Increase Your Wealth*.

My book is what I would call a user-friendly guide to saving tax on your property income. Increasingly, people are investing in property as a way to supplement their savings, but they aren't necessarily taking the right steps from the tax point of view. In actual fact, they are leaving money on the Inland Revenue table, as I call it.

My book is No.1 in its niche. I'm very proud of that, and it's a fantastic business card. There's nothing better than being able to open your presentation with the fact that you're a No.1 bestseller on Amazon and hold the book up so people buy it. It gives you instant authority. I'm also finding that people are now coming to me who have read the book and are wanting more of my services. It was hard work, but it was well worth it.

How much time did you spend writing your book, and how much time did you spend researching it?

Well, I suppose it would not have happened if I hadn't attended your course, which was fantastic. So, thank you very much for that. It was something that I wanted to do, but I didn't really know where to start. I think your course was called 'Write Your Book in 28 Days' but it took me something like 28 weeks because life got in the way! But the process at the start was invaluable, and that enabled me to work through my book gradually. A lot of the knowledge was already there because I've been in practice for a long time. It just needed to be fine-tuned and made user-friendly.

So initially I was writing for a couple of hours every day, setting aside guaranteed time. But then, as always, things get in the way, and you find reasons why you can't do your allotted two hours, which was frustrating. So in the end, I took myself off to Switzerland where we have a house. I locked myself away out there — no e-mails, no telephone, no nothing — and then I just blitzed it. I would get up, write for three hours, have a break, and write for another three hours. Over ten days, it morphed into the first draft of my book.

Did you speak it at any point, or did you just type it?

No, it was typed all the way through.

So tell me about the plotting and structuring process for your book once writing was underway.

Initially I thought, 'If I met somebody at a social event or a networking event, what would they be asking, and who would my target audience be?' So I sort of worked it back from there.

There were a number of taxes that impact on your property income — whether it's income tax, capital gains tax, inheritance tax or possibly corporation tax. So I then put these into the various chapters and thrashed it out. I thought, 'What if I was in my late fifties and had a bigger property, what would I want to be doing and what would my concerns be?' So I went through each generation — whether you're just come out of university, you've got your first job or you've got a bit of money you inherited or whatever — looking at the ways that tax would impact on you and what you could do to avoid it.

So what was the easiest part of writing your book?

I suppose my easiest bits were the most technical bits! That is to say: writing about what is tax deductible and what isn't tax deductible, and giving some examples. Then, I had to put it into non-accountant language. People have always said to me that I'm not your typical accountant. I guess that's because I demystify tax and the language around it, and I then break it into manageable chunks.

I use humour a lot to get the message across — it's not a fun book, but I try to get facts across in a humorous way. People might think, 'My goodness, an accountant who's written a book about tax; that's going to be boring. Why would I want to buy a book about accounts written by an accountant?' It's pleasing that the reviews on Amazon say it's a fun read, and it's an easy read. Somebody in our village bought the book, not because he has any property, but because he was just intrigued that I've written a book. The following week, he said: "I really enjoyed it. It was like having a chat with you in the pub." He said that it was good stuff, but not delivered in an overly complex way.

What were the most challenging parts of writing your book?

Life certainly gets in the way, which is why I went off and blitzed it. Sorting out the title was quite hard work — just making sure that it was be something that would appeal to readers. The artwork was a bit of a challenge too, but we got there in the end. Obviously I had help along the way, so it wasn't just me doing it.

How many alternative titles did you come up with before you decided on *Legally Avoid Property Taxes*?

I had about ten. They were all about avoiding tax. There was an awful lot in the press about avoiding tax: people like Jimmy Carr and Gary Barlow found themselves in some hot water for avoiding tax. It's slightly frowned upon, I suppose, that you're trying to avoid tax. But in reality, there's nothing that says you should sort your affairs to pay as much tax as possible! So my title may upset a few people, but the people I'm aiming the book at actually do want to avoid tax. So in the end, I thought, 'Yes, we need to put it on there.'

How did you choose the artwork and colours for your book cover? How many covers did you look at before you hit on the final one?

I belong to a mastermind group, so I took my covers along there and said, "Look at these — what do you think?" The one we ended up with was one they thought was the best. There's one guy who's very good on graphic design and artistic stuff, so he was very good at advising on colours. I wanted something that was pleasing on the eye and conveyed what the book was all about. The book has quite an aspirational house on the front, and I know it's a bit of a cliché, but it does what it says on the tin. It's bright, it's vivid, the lettering is quite bold.

Within my industry, there are quite a few people who know me, but people aren't necessarily going to look for 'Iain Wallis' on Amazon. But they will be looking for 'avoid taxes.' So it was important to have a cover that didn't necessarily feature me. So it was less about who I was, and more about what the book would do.

You have over thirty years' knowledge about taxes and also about property investment. You could have written about many other different topics. How did you settle on this book?

The reason I chose this one is because it's the thing that I know most about. It's like a lead magnet: it works both for the people I want to help invest in property and also people I want to help save tax. So there's a natural synergy between property and taxation.

While I was writing that book, there were other books I thought of. I thought, 'I quite fancy writing about that' or 'I've got quite a bit of knowledge about that subject.' But did I necessarily want to write a whole book about them? It was certainly a labour of love. But once it's in your hand, it's all worth it. It's quite an emotional moment when you open the first box of books. I just felt it was the ultimate business card.

What have you done in terms of promotion for your book? Are you selling most books on Amazon or are most of your sales offline?

Amazon are selling a reasonable chunk, but they keep selling out. There was one trade show where I spoke on both days, and we sold a good number of copies on both those days. Initially, the trade show was quiet. Then I spoke, and it was like the first day of the Harrods sale; it went absolutely crazy with people trying to get hold of the book. It's got a cover price of £24.99 and £3 of that goes to Cancer Research — but we were knocking them down for £20. It was fantastic.

Then I promoted it myself. We did a lot of work on Twitter and Facebook in all the property groups, LinkedIn as well. Occasionally, we put in some quite controversial titles such as 'Is Your Accountant an Undercover Agent for HMRC?' to sell more books.

So there's lots of stuff we were doing like that, and my P.A. was going up to the post office most weeks posting a load of books. I'm fairly active on Facebook and in a lot of the property groups. I'm always plugging stuff in there, and that's basically how it works. Then I often speak at

156

property networking events, and I'll sell a few there.

The biggest sales have come from Amazon though; I've had two royalty cheques so far.

Are you selling more e-books or physical books?

The physical book. The e-book has had a very painful birth, and that's just being slightly tidied up at the moment. So again, a chance to re-launch the book with the e-version.

How are people finding your book on Amazon? Is it through your promotion and marketing? Or is it being done via keyword searches and SEO [search engine optimisation]?

It's just on SEO — we're not doing any sort of hard promotion. We featured in two magazines and two newspapers, which was good. One was a local newspaper, the other was a trade journal within the property world. I was rather hoping for a snippet in *The Sunday Times* or *The Financial Times,* which would really have turbo-charged sales, but nothing came of that.

You talked earlier about having a conversational tone in your book. When you were writing, did you imagine someone sitting in the same room as you or chatting to one of your clients? How did you emotionally and mentally go through the process of communicating your ideas?

I was imagining I was talking to someone. I'd done a reasonable amount of speaking on property and tax before, so I was quite used to standing up and chatting about it. If you're in a room talking to somebody, their eyes will glaze over if you start getting too technical. They want stuff that they can easily understand and real-life examples that they can relate to. All the examples in the book are situations people have had in their real lives; we're not creating examples for examples sake, they are real-life situations. So it was a case of typing away and out came the book. There was a lot of re-reading and going through it again to take out the jargon. In certain areas, my writing was too technical so that needed to be made more user-friendly.

What sort of feedback have you had from your readers — has this been helpful to you as an author?

It's been great. It's quite humbling when people make the effort to put something on Amazon — taking time out of their life to write a review. That's nice. There's been a couple that have said, "I would have liked a bit more about this," or "I would like a bit more about that," and they've knocked a star off for that. I've gone back to them and said, "Well thank you very much, what could I do to make it a five-star review next time?" My brother was very proud and quite impressed with it, as was my mum. It was hard work, but it's just great to have it.

What sort of impact has it had on you and your business?

I would say *massive*. Just last week, for example, we had three enquiries: one from somebody who had bought the book, has eight properties and wants to buy her partner out, and doesn't know the best way to do it. There were also two other enquiries from people who have got significant wealth through student HMOs, and they don't think their accountant is giving them the best advice. So that was just three enquiries last week. Typically, that will lead to consultations you're paid for. Then, after that, one of two things will happen: either we'll agree to work together or they'll take away the advice and say, "Thank you very much." At least once a week, we'll get an enquiry from somebody who wants us to do a one-off consultation or to give some advice.

Your book came out nearly a year ago. So you didn't have just an immediate impact after the launch, it's been having an ongoing impact ever since?

Yes, it's ongoing. Some people will have bought the book before they contact me. But suppose they come across me on LinkedIn, then my book will come up on Amazon, and you've got instant authority with somebody who doesn't even know you. One fellow wrote and said "Dear Mr Wallis," so he didn't have a clue who I am, but he felt confident enough to make contact with me because of the book and the authority it gives me.

How did you feel when you first started writing? Did you feel daunted by the idea of writing a book?

Yes. It was something I wanted, but I wondered, 'How am I going to fit it in with all the other stuff that goes on in my life.' That was the challenge. I felt I had all the knowledge, given what I do and how long I've been doing it for. But knowing where to start was the hardest part, which is why I came on your course.

How did you make your property book different to all the others on the market? How much time did you put into thinking about this?

There are a number of books on property, so the title was really important. It's a good cover too for attracting people. Also, the blurb about the book, the fact that it's not a tax manual, it's very useful. You should be buying the book no

159

matter where you are on your property journey.

Your cover image is very aspirational and upmarket, rather than say, a picture of a Monopoly board or a terraced house. Explain your thought processes while you were choosing your cover image.

Yes, it's a nice sort of house on the front. People want it. My brother jokes that it's a lot easier playing Monopoly for real than it is on the board game. To be honest, all property owners are, aren't they? They're going round the board collecting properties, collecting rent, refurbishing them, re-mortgaging them, and moving onwards.

I couldn't have a picture of the taxman on the front as it strikes fear into people. Everyone is scared of the taxman. There's no need to be scared of him at all, but that's what keeps accountants in business! A number of property accountants have bought the book, which is quite funny. I'm sure they're just having a little nose to see what's going on. But it's another book sale as far as I'm concerned!

Your sub-title is: '51 Top Tips to Save Property Taxes and Increase Your Wealth.' Do you think it helps having a specific number on your book cover?

Yes, the number is important. There's another book that offers a hundred and one tips. I could possibly expand mine to a hundred and one tips, but fifty-one is better. It's still quite chunky. It enables you develop each point thoroughly. Yes, the number's important: fifty-one sounds better than fifty or forty-nine. There's a whole psychology about choosing the right numbers.

That applies to pricing too. The price of £24.99 is not cheap for a book, but if you can't afford to spend twenty-five quid on a book to help you invest in property, you shouldn't really be investing in property. We decided on that price, and I'm happy with that.

What sort of books do you read? Do you have time to read other authors' books?

Yes, I read a lot of self-development stuff. There's always ways you can sharpen the sword and get yourself doing things better. I read a lot of autobiographies. Sports biographies. Biographies of people in business. On holiday though, I tend to read complete rubbish because I like to switch off and forget about everything. So it tends to be fiction. Ian Rankin's stuff is always quite good — that's the most recent I've bought. Thrillers, that sort of thing.

How did you deal with writing anecdotes about your clients in your book? It's quite a delicate area isn't it — what did you do to disguise them?

I don't use names in the book at all. So what I did was change the numbers, and I changed the names and the gender. So if it was a woman, I would make it a man, and vice versa. We open with the example of a lady who came to me with a large portfolio of property and a limited life expectancy, to give a powerful example of how that would impact on family life. That was an actual case. But there's no way that the person who came to me would ever recognise themselves in my book.

You make a charitable donation to Cancer Research for every purchase of your book. That's quite a big thing for you, isn't it?

Yes, it is a big thing. I try not to burst into tears; it's quite an emotional bit. My sister-in-law died of cancer; she was the same age as me, and she died back in 2003. So for me every year after that is a bonus. My wife and I had just had the best day of our life — which was being in Australia when England won the Rugby World Cup – and two weeks later my sister-in-law was dead. It was a pretty difficult time. So that's basically it. It's one of my preferred charities; it's important for me to give something back.

IDEAS FOR YOU

- There are lots of topics you may fancy writing about. But ask yourself if you would really want to write a *whole* book on them!

- Ask yourself: 'If I met somebody at a social event or a networking event, what would they be asking?' This will give you the chapters and contents for your book.

- Put information into manageable chunks and avoid jargon.

- Use real-life stories and situations to illustrate your points. Change people's names and gender to disguise their identities.

- Try setting aside a couple of hours a day to write your book. If this doesn't work, lock yourself away and write in three-hour blocks for ten days.

- Use humour to get your message across. Make your facts fun.

- Choose a cover that does what it says on the tin. Test out your designs on potential readers.

- Use controversial headlines to promote your book on property groups on Twitter, Facebook and LinkedIn.

- Hold your book up when you give presentations and talks. This will give you instant authority.

- Having a number in your subtitle (such as *51 Top Tips*) can help sales.

- Use sales from your book to help charities close to your heart and give something back.

MICHAEL HOLMES

"The worst point was when someone broke into my car and stole my computer with three un-backed up chapters of my book."

Michael Holmes is bestselling author of *Renovating for Profit* and a respected journalist, broadcaster and property developer.

He's presented many TV programmes including: *Move or Improve?* (ITV), *Good Bid, Good Buy* (ITV), *Trading Up* (BBC), and *I Own Britain's Best Home* (C5).

He's Editor-in-Chief of *Home Building & Renovating*, *Real Homes* and *Period Living* magazines. He's appeared as property expert on *Richard and Judy* and *Tonight* with Trevor McDonald.

He also works as a property investor and developer, with over thirty completed developments.

My book was commissioned in 2004. I've spent about ten years presenting TV programmes. The publisher found me on the back of the TV shows or the pieces I'd written for newspapers. They said: "We'd like you to write a book," and we came up with the title *Renovating for Profit*. The book ended up taking four years to finish simply because I was so busy filming and working on magazines. It was quite a long gestation period with them continually chasing me. So it was a labour of love.

In the end, it was written primarily in stolen time, evenings and weekends, late nights, or when I was meant to be on holiday with my family. They'd be out skiing or at the beach, and I would be either back at home or at best, back at the accommodation writing the book. They do say, "If you want a job doing, give it to a busy person," and it's true. The only way I could do it was in time fitted around all my other activities.

What about the commissioning process? Explain how you chose your topic and book title.

The publishers specifically wanted a book to accompany a sister title they had called *Building Your Own Home* that was a bestseller for self-builders. They wanted a similar book to go alongside this but aimed at the renovation and home improvement market. So they had a very firm idea of which area they wanted to cover. They knew there was a gap in the market. So it was a question of "What shall we call it?" I had written a feature called 'Renovating for Profit' for one of the magazines. It had been on the front cover, and it sold very well. Back then, with 'Property Ladder' being at the height of its popularity, every man and his dog was thinking of getting into buy-to-let or property development as a second career, so it really struck a chord, and I started presenting seminars with the same title,

Renovating for Profit: Adding Space and Value. The seminars were very popular too, so it seemed like a good catchy simple title. It's very much a guide for anybody thinking of doing home improvements. Whether you're doing it to make a profit professionally, or whether you're doing it as a homeowner, you've got to have one eye on ensuring that you're not throwing good money after bad. You want to know you're going to get your money back on your investment.

What sort of impact did your book have when it was published?

It's been a solid seller since it came out. It's managed to stay pretty consistently high in the Amazon sales rankings, apart from one period when the first edition came out of print [Laughs]. Then, there were three to six months when the publisher arranged a second edition. The reviews and the feedback have been very positive, and it's been very well received. It's been fantastic.

It's an achievement of which I am very proud. Everybody feels that they'd like to write a book; probably everybody thinks they've got a good book or two in them, and I'm sure they have. But finding the time to be able to do that is another thing, and mine was definitely written out of stolen time. If it's your heart's ambition to write a book, you *can* do it alongside a very busy life. But it's going to be burning the midnight oil, and it's going to be your weekends and evenings too. At the time, I was looking after three consumer magazines that were probably selling over a hundred thousand copies in the UK; I was filming two TV shows, and I was running a couple of building projects. But I always say, "It's all very well writing about it, but the relevance and pertinence come from actually *doing* it. Anybody can write a theory."

Did your book help you to fill the seats at your seminars? You were running seminars at the same time weren't you?

They feed into each other. It definitely provided a focus for the seminars because I think writing a book forces you to distil your thoughts. Interestingly, the book came out in 2008. It was written primarily in 2006-7, and my Introduction takes a very cautious tone. That was well ahead of the 2007 credit crunch and the ultimate calamity of it really hitting in 2008 when the money dried up for the property sector. I had warned: "This cannot go on forever. When any idiot can buy a property, and it doesn't matter what they do, they're going to make money because the market is going to bail them out, however incompetent they are, it has to end. The market cycle of caution turning to confidence, turning to over-confidence, overheating and bust is inevitable and will happen again. To succeed long term, you need to take a more disciplined approach, a more scientific approach and really understand all the different parameters involved in property investment." What I set out to do was to write a survivors' guide so that when the tough time comes — as it did following 2008 and all of the other booms and busts — those who've read it and taken on board my principles will still survive and not be taken down.

This is with the caveat that it's a one-way market in the UK. Unless there's a major change to the planning system, you cannot lose money on property in this country providing you don't become a forced seller. That remains true, as long as you're not forced to sell your properties in a down-market (which we saw from 2008 to 2010). If you can hang on through those periods and sit tight without over-leveraging and your lenders losing faith and calling in their debt, it will eventually come good. That's exactly what has happened for those who managed to survive the credit crunch. If you sat on your portfolio around 2007 until today, you've got your money back, and if you're in the south and south-east you're going to make more money.

For example, I met a gentleman who invested very, very early in Docklands. He was taken out by one of the 1980s' recessions. I was told that if the banks had not folded on him and forced him to liquidate, he'd now be a multi-millionaire if not a billionaire. I'm sure there are many stories like that. If you over-leverage, you get taken out of the game and can lose a lot of money. But if you're cautious enough not to ever be over-exposed, then you can survive anything. In Britain, property prices are only going to go one way. We're a small island with a growing population, and people will always need somewhere to live. So I do think it's a very secure market long-term providing you can survive those peaks and troughs and adjust your exposure — primarily your debt to asset ratio — during those periods.

You're also Editor of *Homebuilding & Renovating* magazine. Tell me about this publication.

Homebuilding & Renovating magazine is the bestselling title for anybody looking to build an individual home. So it's aimed at self-building and those looking to commission a one-off home. When we say self-build, we don't mean the person who is DIY-building their own home. We're talking about anybody who is going to commission bespoke a one-off house and anybody taking on a major project like a barn conversion, school conversion or a major remodel of their home. So it's a sort of heavy-end residential building project. I'm the Content Director of that magazine alongside the Content Director of *Real Homes* magazine, which is very much for people looking to do home improvements — such as extensions, re-models, loft conversions, basement conversions, garage conversions, extensions and the like, right the way through to kitchen and bathroom updates.

With both these titles, around fifteen per cent of the readership is investor professionals. I also look after the content for *Period Living* magazine, which is for people looking to renovate and improve a period property — so lots of listed properties and pre-1914 properties. Then I am also Content Director of related websites and seven exhibitions called *The Home Building & Renovating Shows* across the UK.

I'm sure that keeps you incredibly busy. Do you think you would write another book?

I would definitely write another book. My book extensively covers your tax position (including the structure of the vehicle you set up to make your investments) the building regulations and the planning system. These things move on quite quickly, so I need to update a new edition of *Renovating for Profit*. I think there's probably room for a broader consumer guide to renovating too — a Renovator's Bible if you like, which is less focused on the 'property investment, property developer' angle and more consumer-orientated. It would be more for the general homeowner who's looking to create something that they're purely going to enjoy living in, with less focus on getting every penny spent to give a return. So it'd be more about creating a bespoke, comfortable, individually-designed home.

Can you share your writing process — whether you plotted your book first or just got on and wrote it.

I knew the structure and planned the whole book in

skeleton form with some detail. Very early on, the publisher wanted a sample chapter and structure, so I knew what I had to write. I didn't write it in sequential order though. I wrote it chapter by chapter, but not in the order it appears. I knew always what Chapter twenty-one would be about; I always knew what Chapter eight would be about. So I wrote it as stand-alone chapters. If you like, each one of these chapters almost stands alone as a 'book' in itself. Certainly, several of these chapters do. Then, they're bound together as one. So you can dip in and out of it, or read a chapter that stands alone, and just look specifically at one aspect of renovating the exterior or renovating the interior or dealing with listed properties.

How did you write it? Did you write it, type it or speak it into a Dictaphone?

I wrote it on an Apple Mac, but I spoke it in my head using my own voice. The worst point in the whole period was when I took my computer to see The Rolling Stones at Twickenham. Whilst I was there, someone broke into my car and stole my computer with three un-backed up chapters of my book. Each one represented probably a fortnight of my life. It was one of the low points in my life. I know that sounds pathetic when you think of some of the things that happen to people, but it was dreadful. However, having written those chapters already, it's remarkable the writing and editing process you've already gone through in your head. I think the re-writes of those chapters were better than the originals. There's something to be said for writing a book, chucking it out, then re-writing the book [Laughs]. Because you've done the research, you've decided what you're going to write, you've done the thought processes, and probably your memory of it is edited in a better way. It's quite hard if you've worked on something for two days to edit it. You just can't do it. You can't be your own editor because you're very reluctant to cut out that fantastic bit you enjoyed writing and in which you think you've imparted some useful tips. Maybe in the bigger scheme of things, it could be edited down. But you don't want to let go of something that you know that you spent a day or so writing. So although those chapters were lost, and it was a dreadful, dreadful moment, my book really benefited from my laptop being stolen.

That's a very positive spin on it. What was your experience of working with a mainstream publisher? How did you find this?

They were essential. If they had not been there with a big stick poking me all the time, it probably would never have got done. I use to dread the calls. "How are you getting on with the book?" "Well, err, I've got another TV series. You'll be delighted: it will be a bigger profile." "But how are you getting on with the book?" They did force me to write it! I had deadlines that slipped and slipped and slipped. But I still had deadlines, and without them I don't think I would ever have delivered it. So Random House/Ebury has a lot to be thanked for.

How many copies has your book sold to date?

From Amazon, it's several thousand, probably fifteen thousand plus, which is a lot for non-fiction.

How do your e-book sales compare with your physical books?

I haven't ever agreed to an e-book. So I signed a book contract with Ebury at Random House. The terms in the original contract were very good. They then subsequently came up with a revised e-book contract that paid me less than the printed version. They were saying I would get less royalties than for the print edition, so I didn't sign it for that reason — if someone wants it they can buy the paper edition. So I'm not in the e-book market; it's hard copies only. I don't know whether I'm right or not, and there would have been more e-book sales than printed version sales. So it could be costing me money!

Do you find many of your clients, or people that come to your seminars, have already read your book before they meet you?

Yes, very much so. Also, lots of people buy it on the back of the seminars. I meet lots of people who have read it, which is very satisfying.

What did you do to market your book and publicise it?

I had various sample chapters in the newspapers. It's not that long ago that *The Sunday Times* Irish Edition ran a big section from it. I've allowed various magazines to serialise small sections of it in exchange for a mention at the end. Then, I've mentioned it at the seminars I've presented over the years. Then, simple things like making sure you've got good reviews on Amazon. My Twitter and Facebook profiles also mention the book. Little things like that all add up.

You chose mainstream publishing for your first book. Would you consider self-publishing for your next one?

Yes, I would. Because you can sell self-published books on Amazon. There's a lot to be said for it now because publishers' power and ability to get you into bookstores has diminished. So I think there's a lot to be said in favour of self-publishing. I think the key question is: would you actually get around to writing it, as there would be no publisher with a big stick? I think a lot of people could make a lot of money self-publishing e-books.

You've had a long career as a property journalist and broadcaster, but you've also completed twenty-eight projects as a property developer ...

I'm now on project twenty-nine to thirty. I'm now renovating a grade-two listed farmhouse and outbuildings for myself, at the same time as project managing a new hotel and leisure complex in Chipping Norton, in Oxfordshire.

Which came first: writing or property development?

My background is journalism, and I was writing specifically about self-build and renovation. I'd always harboured a dream of being able to do that myself. Living in London, opportunities for self-build were few and far between. So we settled for buying a flat and renovating instead. So we bought a property that just needed a bit of a cosmetic makeover on a DIY basis, except for putting a gas fire in. So we proceeded to renovate it and redecorate it. It was very much a lightweight renovation: damp treatment, sanding down of windows and stripping back woodwork. We replaced all of the doors and handles, put down wooden flooring, re-opened the fireplace and had a nice surround and hearth fitted. Then we redecorated throughout.

So it was quite a lightweight cosmetic makeover. But about eighteen months later, we got it valued, and it had gone up significantly in value. This was about 1995 to 1997, and we thought we'd done very, very well. We were desperate to build our own home, so we decided the only way we'd be able to self-build would be to move out of London. My wife is from Oxfordshire, so we chose to move out here where land is more affordable. We used to get the local papers from Oxford delivered to London. So every Saturday morning, we'd get *The Oxford Times* and spend the first hour of the day scanning through looking for building plots.

After several aborted trips up to Oxfordshire, we thought we were never ever going to find somewhere. I think my wife was on the point of giving up when a plot came up that happened to have a nice paddock available next to it. I'd been writing about property for about five years already by then, so I realized the potential to combine this paddock and this small building plot into a half-acre building plot. So instead of the small four-bedroom house that had planning permission, we'd be able to build a much bigger six-bedroom house. Also, the bigger plot would allow it to be rotated to face due south to look out over the fields; it would, therefore, be a much grander, more attractive property. So we bid for the plot and were lucky enough to get it and built our first house. So we started out as self-builders. We stretched ourselves financially, knowing that to get the optimum gain you really need to build the right house for the plot.

So anyone who's thinking of doing a project like this, you've got to weigh up your own needs and requirements and your financial position alongside, "If I'm going to buy this property, what's the optimum thing to do with it?" To buy a very large plot or a very large property, and not have enough budget to be able to do it justice, is a mistake. So you need to be able to deliver the optimum outcome. Or, at least if you can't do it all in one phase, to ultimately aim to be able to deliver the optimum property for that site based on a balance of your own requirements and what you think the sale potential would be. So in this instance, we stretched ourselves financially and set out to build it.

We started with two people, both with incomes, both with jobs, and in the process our first child came along. So, suddenly, we went down to one income and had an extra mouth to feed. By the time we moved in (it took just over a year to build it, about six months in planning) and lived there for a year, our second child arrived. So we went from two incomes and no kids to one income and two kids, and we realized we'd better put this house on the market. We initially expected the house to be worth around £475,000 but it went to a bidding war and sold for around three-quarters of a million pounds. That made us wake up to the potential of investing in property; as a second career really, alongside journalism.

Do you think your readers relate to you because you're an 'ordinary person' who became a property developer — so it seems possible for them too?

Yes, that's probably right. I'm still doing it, still suffering, still learning. The nature of the business always throws up new challenges. You've never learnt it all. Every building is different and every situation is different; whether it's legal challenges or planning challenges or solutions to meet building regulations. Whether it's just the things that life throws at you with ground conditions or the weather. There are always new challenges, so it's never dull. I think it's the fact that I've actually done it myself. I think it's one of the true ways of self-improvement to get engaged in building your own home and renovating a home for yourself and your family. It really is about self-betterment!

Has it ever been a choice for you: property journalist or property investor? Or are the two too bound up together?

The two are very bound together. I love writing, so I'd hate to give that up. I do enjoy being in the media world. I've enjoyed doing television; it's bought me opportunities that have also enriched my life and been great fun and experiences.

They do feed off one another. I think to be a writer and not do it makes you irrelevant. There are lots of people who write about it, but you can tell they don't actually do it. Yes, I could just go and be a developer or an investor, and I think one day that might be the case. But I'm sure I'll still have one hand in the media as well.

IDEAS FOR YOU

- If you have a hectic schedule, write your book in stolen time — burn the midnight oil or use weekends. You *can* do it alongside a busy life.

- Consider holding seminars that tie in with your book if you're not doing so already. Your book and your seminar will feed into one another.

- Choose a book title that strikes a chord with your readers.

- Plan the structure of your book in skeleton form before you start writing. Fill in the detail later.

- Don't worry about writing in a sequential order.

- Write chapters so that each one almost stands alone as a 'book' in itself, so the reader can dip in and out.

- It's hard to be your own editor and let go of something you've spent two days writing.

- Allow magazines to serialise small sections of your book in exchange for a credit at the end.

- There's a lot to be said for self-publishing now that traditional publishers' power has diminished.

- Building regulations, taxes, and the planning system are constantly changing. So update the contents of your book and bring out a revised edition if necessary.

- Writing and business feed into each other. There's no need to choose one at the expense of the other.

SAMANTHA COLLETT

"It boosted my profile and got me great coverage with The Times."

Samantha Collett is an award-winning landlord, property investor, auction addict, and former letting agency owner.

She is a bestselling author of *How to Buy Property at Auction* and *Property Investment: The Essential Rules*, published by Constable & Robinson

A columnist with *Estates Gazette* and *Evening Standard Homes & Property,* Sam is also a multi-award winning blogger for WhatSamSawToday.com on Primelocation.com, which has been featured in *The Daily Telegraph's* top property blogs.

She has forty-three properties worth several million pounds all around the UK.

I've been writing a blog for about four years now. I used to have a letting agency business, which I had sold at the end of 2012. I was going to take a year's sabbatical and do a bit of travelling. I met with an author friend, who is massively successful with about fifty books out, and she said to me, "I think you should write a book on property auctions because you've been writing about it on your blog. Obviously, you've got interest as your blog's been growing." I'd never thought of that before, so I decided to look into it.

So I put it all together. Then, I met another of my friends who knows how to talk to me about reality. I said, "I'm thinking of doing this book, and I'm going to self-publish it." He said I needed to get a publisher rather than self-publish. So I sent e-mails to a few publishers, who I thought would be appropriate.

I contacted a little publisher called How To Books, and they said, "Yes, we would like your idea." I didn't hear from them for a couple of months, then it turned out they had been acquired by Constable & Robinson. They e-mailed me out of the blue and said they were going to take my proposal to an acquisitions meeting that was in a few days' time.

In the meantime, I had already written the book because I thought I wasn't going to wait around; I just wanted to get on with it. When they said they wanted to buy it, I said, "Good because I've written it. Here's the book." So they took it, and it took about a year to publish. With me coming from a blogging background where I write something, and it's online in seconds, I found the whole process quite slow.

The copy editor said, "It's a joy to read, but you use 'which' a bit too much so I've taken out a few of them. I hardly did anything to it so that your voice comes across."

So I was really chuffed about that. That was tremendous as it is actually the first "how to" book out there in terms of "how to buy a property at auction." It's crazy because the property auction market is worth billions of pounds and people have been doing this sort of thing for years, but I've actually written a book about it.

I love what I do. I've always encouraged people to go to the auction room to buy property. That's why I write for the *Estates Gazette* magazine as well, which is the property industry bible. I haven't got enough money to buy everything: loads of properties go to auction, and there are some great projects. I love tweeting and sharing with people.

I've been doing this for years before I even started writing my blog. For years, I used to bore my friends to death every week with my top tips for auctions. When you have a little obsession — the same way you want to make better writers out of people — I want to encourage people to come to the auction room and to experience it. So you share your own passion.

I finished *How to Buy Property at Auction* in about March, and I got payment in advance of fulfilling the contract. Then, in September/October that same year, the editors invited me to lunch. They said, "We want you to write a book on buy-to-let." I said, "No, there is already an author out there who has written a bible on buy-to-let. So unless I'm going to write something that's better or different, I'm not going to get into that space." They were very surprised by that. I have a very different style of writing to David Lawrenson, but fundamentally he has written a fantastic book, so I just wasn't going to do that. I said, "I will write you my rules of property investment. We can make it nice and bite-size because I think people have a short span of attention nowadays." So they agreed to that.

They originally told me it would be published in November 2014, and this was a conversation we were having in September/October 2013. But I said, "No, I want it out in July," because I wanted to get into the summer holiday reading market. As it turned out, my original title got lost, and it became a more Google-friendly title, as I understand. But I managed to keep the orange cover for it, which I fought long and hard for. It's called *Property Investment: The Essential Rules*.

Your book covers are important to you, aren't they? Tell me more about your negotiations with the publisher.

That was one of the key conditions when I wrote the second book. As an author, you feel quite precious about your book, and I didn't feel that the cover of my property auction book was right for the contents. It didn't reflect my writing style. That was quite difficult for me to reconcile. When they asked me to write the second book, I said, "The only way that you'll get me on board is if I can have more creative control." As you know from the contract, Stephanie, they're the ones who get the last say.

So, explain what happened with the second book cover.

I had always envisaged this book would be orange because to me orange represents freshness, and I felt this was a fresh perspective on property investment. I'm pleased to say I managed to keep orange on the cover. I didn't want my face, and at least they didn't put any images on there, as they were trying to do. It was quite a fraught time. You don't always realize how important the cover is to you as an author. You write the book and then you suddenly realise, "That's not what I want." I think because you're so busy writing the words, you don't realise that you won't have any control over what the book is going to look like.

The discussions can be massively distracting for a writer, as you know. They said they wanted the book finished by December, and we were having this meeting mid-October, so I had six weeks to write it. I was fed up with having all these discussions about what it looked like. That's why I went looking for an agent because I didn't want to be weighed down by it. I just thought, 'Let me get on and do what I'm good at; someone else can fight these battles.' Luckily, I'm now working with an amazing agent.

You also had to consider whether you should use Sam or Samantha for your books in the male-dominated property market. Tell me about those discussions.

That was with my editor for my *Auction* book. The funny thing is that I am mainly known as Sam because my blog is under What Sam Saw Today (www.whatsamsawtoday.com) and I use Sam Collett everywhere. It's not Samantha, which sounds very formal and feels a bit like the 1980s for me. So we had this conversation about, "Should I keep my name uniform, or should it be like a stamp in the ground that I am a woman, and that is a good thing?" We were considering whether it was a strength or a weakness to use "Sam." In the property industry, and especially in auctions, it's a very male world, and you have to ask yourself: are your readers potentially going to be put off because you're a woman? Or will it be a positive thing? You and I were talking about how many of your case studies so far have been men, so is it good to be a role model and state that you are explicitly female to attract other women or does that somehow say something else? I don't know.

It's funny. I know that from my blog I've got way more male readers than female. Reflecting on this, maybe it's a little bit silly to think that in any way people would respect me less because I'm a woman property investor. I don't know. With men in property, there seem to be cock fights all the time: "How big is your Ferrari?" "How big is your house?" etc.

I am probably quite different to a lot of property people in the fact that I value time much more than I do money, which means that I live my life in a different way. I have a nice car, but I don't have the latest Ferrari, and I haven't got a massive house or anything like that. I am not prepared to work a hundred and twenty hours a week to do it. I do stuff because I think it's going to be fun, so when you start from that premise, it just means that you live life how you choose. Money doesn't turn me on. Once you've got a nice house, you've got gas and electric, you've got food on the table, and you can have a couple of glasses of nice wine, what else do you need? It's fringe benefits — there are only so many fancy restaurants I can go to.

Let's talk about your publishing deal in more detail. A lot of people might be daunted by the idea of having to write a book to a six-week deadline — explain how you did that.

Well, I wake up early in the morning. I normally get up about 5 a.m., so that usually gives me a head-start on people. When I am writing, my family don't really like me because I get into a kind of bubble, and I get up about 3 a.m. I won't have the Internet on, and I turn my phone off for days on end. I just write. I don't really like talking to anyone, and I'll write from 3 a.m. to about 10 o'clock at night.

That's a long working day. How long does it take you to finish your first draft?

It doesn't take me very long at all. I am a fast writer, and my first draft was actually ninety to ninety-five per cent done in that time. I think maybe because I know my subject, it makes it much easier.

Many of my clients are busy professionals or entrepreneurs, and they tend to get their books written in around one to three days. People who've never done it don't believe it's possible, or they worry it might be a lesser book because it's written so quickly.

Once you have a story to tell, it doesn't take you very long. I look at *How to Buy Property at Auction,* and I can't believe what a tremendous book I did. It's so flipping useful and full of information. I look at it and think, 'Does anybody else realise how quickly it was written?' I firmly believe that once you have a story to tell, and you know your subject, you know what needs to be done to get out there. For the first auction book, I knew everything inside out because it was based on what I do on a daily basis. I couldn't wait to share it, and I wanted to inspire people, so I was massively excited. I love to hear back from people who I've helped. It's marvellous.

Let's wind back a little now. Many first-time authors feel nervous about pitching a book idea to publishers, especially when the book hasn't been written. When I tell them to approach a publisher direct, they find all sorts of reasons why they can't do it. They say: "I've never been published before," or "I'm not well-known enough," or "I don't have a literary agent," etc. Your own thought processes are very different aren't they?

People procrastinate and make excuses. The key thing is that I put forward a business plan for the book. I knew what other titles were out there, and I knew my market. So, for example, I knew that there were around 1.4 million landlords in the UK, and I knew how many properties were sold at auction, I knew the membership of the landlord organisations, and the trade magazines, so I could show there was an appetite for something like this.

I did research on other book titles in the market, so I knew who my potential competitors were, even if they were crappy little free books. It's a business proposition at the end of the day. When you're going to a publisher, you know it will probably cost them at least £5,000 to get your book edited and so on. So you have to put together a little sales pitch that says, "This is why you should buy this from me." It's not difficult if you believe in your book, and you believe you can do it. The problem is Stephanie that most people believe that they can't do it. Or they like the idea of doing these things but aren't prepared to put in the extra effort. For example, I am really busy all the time, and I should have taken that sabbatical after I sold my business, but you've got to constantly ask yourself, "Do I want to watch TV or do I want to pull my finger out of my ass and actually do something?" So I get up early in the morning because I want to achieve something; I want to know that I've done something worthwhile today.

I know all these answers, but it's nice hearing someone else say them. [Laughs]. You mentioned the frustrating delay between finishing writing your book and it being published. What did you do in that time in between?

While I was waiting, I spent two months planning a massive launch party. My publishers did not want to back me on this launch party for various reasons, saying they don't work, etc. I thought, 'Fine, I've got enough money. I'll pay for my own launch party.' I booked this lovely private members club with a roof terrace in Marble Arch that I had seen advertised in The Society of Authors' magazine. I didn't want to have it in a bookstore or one of those boring hotel function rooms like everybody else does. I did a deal with the private members club and had a massive launch party. It was awesome for the book — it boosted my profile and got me great coverage with *The Times.*

So you could have taken the view that there was no point having a launch party. But instead you took quite an innovative and imaginative approach. Let's go into the detail of your launch party since this was such a successful launch.

Well, I decided that we should have a live charity auction at my book launch party. I got the top eight property auctioneers in the country all in one room, which had never been done before. I called them all up, and I said, "You need to come and work for free, and you're going to sell off these lots. I am going to get people to donate these lots and then sell them off for charity."

I had selected St Mungo's, which is a homeless charity because there were going to be loads of property investors in the room. I picked St Mungo's as I believe in their work, especially with the rehabilitation and giving homeless people new skills. They don't look down on people with drink and drug problems — they just take the view that crap happens in life. I really want to support their work, so I convinced people to give prizes. Even some of the auction houses and some of those who had already given their time for free, I also convinced to give prizes. It was fantastic. The charity auction lasted just over half an hour, and we raised just shy of £4,000.

I love that — that's something to be proud of. Now, for many authors, it would be their ultimate dream to get a mention in *The Times*. Tell me how you managed to get bloggers and journalists interested whereas other authors struggle?

Because I am a ballsy bitch basically! It doesn't matter how many times you say, "No," I will continue to ask. I am like a dog with a bone. The more you tell me "No," the harder I will push.

Initially, I sent an e-mail to all these random e-mail addresses asking journalists to come along to my event. I just asked them non-stop and wouldn't take, "No" for an answer. I kept contacting everyone and refused to give up. I had no pride!

There were other positive benefits weren't there of raising the money for St Mungo's?

Yes, St Mungo's were very happy with the support and promotion from the book launch event — especially given that I work in the property industry. The money I made for them is very small fry, but it was the connections they made that they were thrilled with. I continue to support them, and they continue to invite me to events. Just last month I went to a St Mungo's event where Kate Adie was giving a talk – oh my God, she is amazing!

Kate Adie was talking about her new book, so I took my agent with me. We were having a few drinks beforehand, and Phil Spencer from the TV show *Location, Location, Location* was there. I thought, 'I want a selfie with Phil. I could tweet it or Facebook it.'

Phil was standing across the room talking to the Chief Executive from St Mungo's. So I went over there and said, "Excuse me — I know you're the Chief Executive, but I really need a selfie with Phil." My agent was so embarrassed, but she took a great photo, and I tweeted it. Then, I had one with Kate Adie afterwards. My agent said, "You are bloody incorrigible, you really are." So it's all about having no pride and persevering!

So a big part of promoting your books is believing in yourself and putting yourself out there.

Yes, and friendliness. I don't get trolls or people trying to take me down online, though you expect to when you put your head above the parapet. I am so fortunate. I don't think I am The Big I Am: I make mistakes and am more than willing to admit them. I openly say, "This is the money I've lost on property: this is the deal that I screwed up, this is what I learned, and this is how you can do it better. I don't pretend to be somebody I'm not. What you see is what you get: I drink too much; I laugh too much. There is no hidden agenda with me, and I am brutally honest. I think now because I've been blogging for such a long time, my life is an open book. You can Google me and find out whatever you want, and if it's not there you can e-mail me, and I will tell you! [Laughs]

How many e-mails are you getting every day now? A lot of people worry about the time factor of blogging and social media.

I get loads of e-mails — I love it. To think that someone is interested enough in what I have to say to send me an e-mail, is wonderful. People are so busy these days, and if someone goes to the trouble of leaving a comment on your blog or if they go to the effort of sending an e-mail, you should be grateful.

What kind of impact have your books had on your life?

Well, my properties are far more lucrative. But the funniest thing is that you could take away all my properties, and I would be happy with my books even if they earned me a tenner. It's that sense of accomplishment. So many people say, "I'm going to write a book," or "I've got a book in me," but most people don't actually do it. So, I'm mega-proud that I've actually done it. *How to Buy Property at Auction* is very close to my heart. It was my first book, and it was like having a child. I feel damn proud of that book because it is really informative. *Property Investment: The Essential Rules* was a real challenge and to get all my management knowledge and ideas into a readable format is a massive accomplishment. When I actually got the book, I was in floods of tears. I remember saying to my partner, "Look how this has totally changed my life." It's massively important to me. My books mean more to me than my houses.

You're a columnist for *Estates Gazette and the Evening Standard Homes and Property Supplement.* That came about as a result of your books too didn't it?

Well, you know when the publisher sends you that form and you have to fill it in about how are you going to promote your book? I was filling it in, and it asked things like: are you going to contact your local newspaper? So I was hemming and hawing about this, and I said, "You know what I should do is get a column in *Homes and Property.*"

So I tracked down the Editor of the *Evening Standard Homes & Property.* Well obviously, I couldn't get through

— they wouldn't let me speak to her — but I did manage to get her e-mail address. So I sent her a punchy e-mail, and I said how awesome the paper was, and she could raise the bar on their awesomeness by including me, and here are some reasons why she should do it. I didn't send any examples of my writing; it was just an e-mail. Then twenty minutes later, she sent back an e-mail saying, "You sound interesting, come and see me."

So I went to see her, and it was a bit scary; I mean she is an incredibly powerful woman. We had coffee, and she said something like, "So you're the little thing who's walked off the street to see me." I was a little annoyed about this. She is very preened, with very perfect blonde hair and everything about her is perfect. Whereas I am not one of those perfect women; no matter how hard I try, I will never be like that.

She asked if I had been to journalism college. I told her, "I haven't – though I have a successful blog, and I've got this book coming out next year." She said, "Well, I've got all these award-winning reporters ..." So I said, "They don't know anything about property auction, but I do." She asked what magazines I had written for. Of course, I said, "None." She asked if I'd had any other training. So, I said, "No." Then, she asked if I'd want paying and I said, "*You* wouldn't work for free." So eventually, she agreed to give it a try.

With the *Estates Gazette*, it was also to do with my book launch. I knew that people did video trailers for their books, so I thought that would be cool. I didn't know how to film or edit it, so I needed to keep it simple. I decided to do a recipe for property auction pie. The twist being I found a company who had a puppet chef — and so I used them to produce my trailer. I know it probably sounds a bit crazy and random — but it did all make sense!

So I did that video, and then I sent it to an auctioneer. He started laughing and thought it was so funny. He was on the phone to the *Estates Gazette,* and he mentioned, "Have you seen the crazy video that Sam has done for her property auction book?"

I had been trying to get into the *Estates Gazette* for years and years and years because they are the industry bible: if you manage to get into that, you've made it. I kept phoning them, and they kept ignoring me up to that point. The auctioneer said, "I hope you don't mind, I've just given the Estates Gazette your phone number as they want to talk to you." So shortly after that, they phoned and said, "What you've done is brilliant. How would you like to write for us?" I couldn't believe it. Anyway, I wrote something for them and sent it over. I was absolutely chuffed when they said they liked it. Then they told me, "Obviously we'll pay you, as we need you to write for us more often. Are you up for it?" I said, "That sounds marvellous, thank you very much." We then went to lunch and had a bottle of wine, and that was it!

So again, it's about people. People buy people. You've got to be good at what you do, and you've got to be passionate. The video I made and the launch party I had weren't just about the book. I love what I do, and I do it because it's going to be fun. It's not because I think to myself, 'How many books can I sell? How much money can I make?' That is not fundamentally how I operate. If you really love what you do, you don't really care if you get paid for it or not. You do it because it's going to be fun, and maybe some other people will like it as well.

I am not your shy retiring wallflower, which is fortunate. I don't mind if I get things wrong. It's amazing how many people want to be a success without taking the necessary steps and without taking action. You have to get up and do it. I don't like this "entitlement" attitude that some people have. You should never rest on your laurels. There's always something fresh to do.

That's a refreshing attitude. If only everyone could be like that! Tell me how you got into property and auctions in the first place.

I quit my marketing job because I wanted to do something of my own. I had also seen the money I made was pipsqueak compared to the directors of the company. I decided to buy a property to do up and make money. My father was very against it as he said, "You aren't a builder!" I had gone to university and got a First Class degree, a Masters, topped off with a Diploma in Advertising — a dream, well-paid job — and then was quitting my career just three years on!

I found this property in Cambridge, and even to this day I can't remember how I found it. That property was being sold at auction. So I bought it, and I still own it to this day. I loved the auction — it was so simple and easy — so I just kept going back time and again. I reckon something like ninety-four per cent of the properties in my portfolio have been bought at auction. I have a property on the market now, which I am selling through the estate agent. It's not an auction property, so it can take weeks to sell. Unfortunately, you can get messed about until the day you exchange. With auction, it's different — if you go and put your hand in the air and keep it there long enough to buy a property, twenty-eight days later it is yours. Sometimes, it can be fourteen days. You can actually plan for builders to come in if you need to get work done. With an estate agent, it goes on and on, and it's difficult to make plans.

Anybody who has ever bought a property at auction will always go back. You get addicted to it. It's so convenient, and you can get a bit of a bargain. You haven't got the stress that comes when you're with an estate agent. You do all your research, and you get all the legal packs beforehand. You just go along, bid and buy, and that's that.

You do it once, and you get the bug. You go and look at a property, then you go for lunch and work out your budget and estimates. It's a marvellous lifestyle.

What are your plans for your next book?

For now, the main thing that keeps me busy is my new project to Biddsy, which is the world's first property auction App. Basically, if people want to buy a property at auction in the UK, I am creating an App where people can get all of that property auction information. People don't realise this, but there are hundreds of auction houses in the UK, and it's so difficult to find property auction information. What I want to do is bring all this information to people in an easy, comfortable way. If you see a property you like the look of, the App will let you see exactly where it is, add auction dates to your diary, and you can contact the auctioneer straight away.

It has been a whole new learning curve, but it is a labour of love. It's crazy: there's around 100 properties per day that go to auction, but people don't know about them. It's such a massive opportunity in this day and age to actually bring new information to people, and put it all together in a nice easy way. I can't wait — I love it!

IDEAS FOR YOU

- Contact publishers who you think may be suitable for your book and pitch your idea to them.

- Put together a business plan to prove there is an appetite for your book.

- If you sign with a mainstream publisher, expect to lose some creative control as they will have the final say over your book title and cover.

- There may be a twelve-month delay before your book is published with a mainstream publisher.

- A literary agent can negotiate with a publisher on your behalf and fight your battles for you.

- Present your information in bite-size chunks as people have a shorter attention span these days.

- A first draft can be ninety per cent written in under twenty-four hours if you know your topic inside out.

- Consider combining your book launch with a creative event such as a live auction to raise money for charity.

- Be persistent when approaching journalists for publicity. Refuse to take "no" for an answer.

- If you'd like to have a regular column in a publication, send the editor a punchy email listing reasons why they should pick you.

- Produce a fun video to promote your book on YouTube.

- People buy people. Be passionate and love what you do — it's infectious!

JAHLYN KING

"Instead of telling ten nurses a week what I do and giving them tips, I could put it all into a book!"

Jahlyn King is author of *Lucky Pennies: Spend One, Save One.*

She has a portfolio of properties worth nearly £1 million in London, which she built up while working as a nurse.

She bought her first home using the council's right-to-buy scheme and made her first £50,000 "by accident" while struggling to earn £1,500 a month as a nurse.

She wrote her book while travelling on the Tube to and from work each day, sometimes after fourteen-hour nursing shifts.

Since becoming an author, Jahlyn has featured in a Channel 5 documentary about people who have bought their council properties on the right-to-buy scheme.

My mind never stops ticking really. There are times on the Tube on the way to work where I've thought, 'Here's something else that could help somebody' or 'This is a tip I've used to look for my latest property.' So I'd write it on a piece of newspaper that I was reading, tear it off and put it in my handbag to write down properly later.

On the ward, once the patients were asleep, there wasn't much to do. All my colleagues would be reading magazines, talking on their mobile phones or snoozing in the chairs. I'd be writing my book then. I'm old-fashioned, so I'm a great fan of pen and paper. So, for example, many chapters of my book were written by hand on the train on the way to a Property Investors' Party. London to Birmingham gave me a good two hours, so I sat there with a notebook, and I just wrote as much content as I could cram in. I tried to make the most of the uninterrupted time because life was hectic at home with working full-time and the latest property search.

What inspired you to want to write your book in the first place?

I was in the middle of a very long shift at work. I should have been finished by about 4 p.m. My mum was cooking dinner, and I expected to be there for about 6 p.m. to join her. I was looking forward to spending time with my mum. But there was a problem at work, and I couldn't leave until about 9 p.m. because there was no other nurse to take over from me. So I had to stay behind, and I missed dinner.

When I got home that night, I was really angry. I thought, 'There's got to be more to life than this. I've worked twelve hours already, and it still wasn't enough; I still couldn't get home and spend time with my mum.' Mum said, "Don't worry, we can put the food in the fridge." But that wasn't the point. It was like work was taking over my life. I couldn't even manage to have a simple meal with my mum. I began to resent my job. I felt shackled to be honest, and I hated it.

There was a little voice in my head that said, "This is why you must save. This is why you must study every night. This is why you must invest in property so you can become free — physically, mentally, spiritually and, of course, financially".

That's what I wrote in my diary that evening. I was writing down my feelings through my frustration and tears — I just let it all out on paper, and I never stopped writing. One page turned into three, which soon became ten. Then I realised that after about seventeen thousand words, I might actually have something that could help other people.

So your personal diary formed the basis for your book. Were you worried about exposing yourself when writing your book?

All the struggles I've had in my property career, and in my nursing career, are there in the book. In my journey as a nurse and as an investor, I am very authentic. I speak from the heart, and I am very down to earth. I just say it how it is, and I hope that I'm able to reach more people by doing that. In my book, there are amusing little anecdotes about my patients or about my love life. I'm not just this property person who goes out and buys property. So hopefully that comes across. People can ask me any question, and I will always answer it honestly.

How did you turn a diary into something that other people would want to read?

The diary kind of showed me the reason why I invest: to become freedom. I've always disliked having a manager telling me what to do or having a rota telling me what shifts to work. Also, I wanted to stay at home when I have a family. I wouldn't have to hand my baby over to a childminder because I would be able to live on my passive income from my property investments.

I'm not saying I'm a multi-millionaire because I'm obviously still working, but I'm well on track to achieving all my personal and financial goals now. More importantly, I don't have to be a multi-millionaire before I can turn round and help the people that are coming up underneath me. What I'm saying is, "This is what I've done. I can leave you some paper breadcrumbs. If you do wish to follow me, just do what I do." We have a duty to help each other. There's room at the top for many of us!

There are some very sophisticated ways of investing that can drive you crazy, very flash ways, very complex ways. It doesn't have to be that difficult; I've just shown my simple way. You can still be a really good investor with just basic maths and a bit of common sense. Wealthy people are not always more intelligent than poorer people. But they'll spend their money on getting a good broker or solicitor. You don't have to be a jack of all trades — you don't have to know everything about property law or mortgages but invest in the already existing experts and develop a team around them. So a staff nurse or teacher can do very well if she has a good team of specialised people around her. Some people think the key is to save money and do it all yourself, but you are not an expert in all the different aspects of property investing; therefore, it's wrong to try and save money here. So it's little nuggets like that really. I'm here to say, "I'm a nurse. I've done it, and I'm still doing it. So you can do it as well." This is the essence of my story, really.

Your book's unusual in that you've included over 100 illustrations and sketches you've done yourself. Tell me about these.

When I was a young girl, I was good at science, and I was very good at art. I remember one of my teachers telling me, "You're going to have to decide whether to go with art or science." I always wanted to be a midwife — that was my dream — so I went with the science. But I never lost my passion for art.

When I started nursing, I gave up the art. I just didn't have the time or the energy. So when I was writing my book, I thought that my readers needed something to look at. Then I thought, 'I love cartoons; I can draw.' In my diary, I doodle too. So this is just like my diary, only I'm doodling with more purpose. It's easy for me to draw. It's when I feel alive and at my happiest. I still have loads of pictures that I haven't been able to include as you have to know when to stop! It was great fun drawing myself in cartoons, and I would have a good giggle sketching out different scenarios.

It's a light-hearted book with a serious message about property investment. Why did you decide on this tone?

I think people like that as it shows you're human. It's nice to have a bit of, "I'm still looking for Mr Right who hasn't turned up yet … but hey, I'm onto my next property!" Life does get in the way, and life can be tough. But you still have to get on and work towards the future — whether you've had a heartbreak or your job's getting you down or something really traumatic happens. In my book, I've got a little illustration of me climbing up the side of a mountain with a pickaxe saying, "It's grit and determination that will get you to the top."

There are also little quotes in the book that I've read over the years and jotted down in my diary that have kept me going. Some of these sayings are quite clichéd, but they still have a good meaning behind them. There are lots of other tips in there, as well.

What's appealing for me is that I can show other nurses certain areas that they can afford to invest, even though it's a little one-bedroom studio. Once they understand the 'how to' and 'why they should' the penny drops if you like, and they are like a greyhound out of the trap. The light goes on in their eyes, and they think, 'I've got something to strive for now.' That's really rewarding. Hearing their progress updates warms my heart and makes me smile. I love it.

Is your book aimed largely at nurses and people in the NHS?

It's aimed at anyone who is half awake in "the matrix." These people know that they know they're not happy in their daily life; they know that there is a better way out there; they know they don't want to work under a boss forever. It's for anybody really — whether you're a nurse, a builder or a schoolteacher that has enough fire in their belly and wants to escape the rat race.

It doesn't have to be property; you can invest in a lot of other things. It's about finding your investment and going

204

for it. I always say that property is the best one as it has the best track record. But if people are interested in other things, just find your passion and invest.

Tell me about your title *Lucky Pennies* and how you chose that. There's quite a poignant story behind this isn't there?

The "pennies" came from when I was a little girl. I used to go to my aunt's house every Sunday and polish her ornaments for a few pennies. I was quite a chubby child and very fond of sweets like most children. After I had completed the polishing, she would give me a few pennies and ask me, "What are you going to do with them?" I'd say, "I'm going to buy some penny sweets." One day she said to me, "No you're not. You're going to spend one and save one." I thought that was really cool because I was still sitting there on her doorstep eating those sweets, and I still had a penny. That's how I learned to save. So now, even when I've just bought a new property, I start saving for the next one automatically.

On the evening I missed the dinner with my mum, there was a song playing on my iPod called '*Any Lucky Penny*' by Sixpence None the Richer. So I thought, '*Lucky Penny: How to Save Yourself Rich.*' It was kind of: save yourself by saving for yourself! It's like a rubber ring to save yourself, so you can float along passively in the future. It's got many meanings, and people still come up with other meanings for what it means to them.

Tell me about the challenges you have experienced along the way while writing your book.

Initially, I thought I'd struggle with the amount of words. I think I came to you at twenty-seven thousand words, and you told me I needed to be nearer seventy thousand. I thought I was going to have a heart attack! [Laughs] Then you gave me some tips about what to expand on, and I looked at it again, and the words came in leaps and bounds.

Getting the pictures done was another challenge. You can't rush drawings, and I wanted to draw them all myself. Scanning those pictures was a nightmare. I didn't have a scanner at the time. I would be in the public library using a scanner machine, trying to scan eighty-four pictures within the hour. I could never do them, so the timer would cut off mid-scan. It would delete all the pictures I'd already sent before! Then it would switch itself back on but under a different setting, so some of my pictures were now being scanned smaller, with different shades and different pixels. To make matters worse, I only knew this once you e-mailed me to say what on earth had happened to some of the pictures when they arrived at your end! So I had to re-book the scanner at the library and travel back down there. Sometimes this was after a night shift, so that was very tough. How many times I walked to that library with tears streaming down my face through utter frustration and exhaustion with Mum on the end of the mobile telling me to keep going and that it would all be worth it in the end. Of course, like all mums, she was completely right!

The other thing that drove me crazy was the Contents page. I would have the Contents ninety-five per cent complete, then I would spot an error in the book. Making this small change — adding a paragraph for example — would sometimes push the existing text onto the next page, which now meant my Contents page needed to be re-worked again because what was on previously on page fourteen was now on page fifteen. This was a nightmare as everything has to be moved down by one page, and it would happen over and over. I screamed a few times and ate far too much chocolate while sorting out the Contents page. I now realise that this can all be done automatically!

What have been the highlights — the best moments?

Actually seeing my cover. It felt like, "Wow! That looks like something I could see in a shop." That really was amazing.

Even before that, when I had gone past the amount of pages that a diary can hold, and I thought, 'What am I doing here?' People often say, "Help me. Tell me how to invest. Say that again, write it down." Instead of telling ten nurses a week what I do and giving them tips, I could put it all into a book and maybe it would help them. When that light bulb first flickered on was a nice point.

Another highlight was getting to eighty-two thousand words. I remember the weekend when I saw that. I stopped then and I left it. The next day, I came back and read it from beginning to end. I laughed, I cried, and I thought, "Wow, I've done this!'

Also, telling other people about my book and seeing their faces as they asked, "What's it about?" It was great; I loved it.

More recently, when the book popped through the letterbox in early October. I'd just got home from my fourth night shift. I was achy and tired and had been home for about ten minutes when the postman started struggling trying to post a package through the letterbox. He could have knocked, and I would've open the door, but I stood on the other side, amused as he kept on shoving in a package that was slightly too big for the letterbox. It finally flew through the door and landed at my feet. I tore it open, and it was my book. Covers, pictures, graphs and diagrams — oh, it was beautiful! To hold that book in my hands was a moment I'll never forget. I flicked to the Contents page and then I cried happy, relieved tears — then lay on my bed with it and fell asleep!

Has it helped to have a mentor — someone to give you feedback — while you've been producing your book?

A thousand per cent. Sometimes I felt so silly asking, "What does this mean or that mean?" So you've explained things along the way, which has been fantastic. The biggest help so far was when I came to visit you, and you gave me a kind of flow chart of what self-publishing was on one side and traditional publishing on the other. It gave me an overview. I felt in my heart that I wanted to go with self-publishing.

When I gave you my first twenty-seven thousand words, you went through it and arrowed bits. You said, "Expand this; leave that bit out." It was having someone else's eyes on my work for the first time, and how you were looking at it. The bits that you thought were great, I didn't think people would be interested in. There were other bits I didn't really need to go to town on as they were less important. That was so valuable.

The strategies you gave me in terms of turning my book into a bestseller. I didn't know anything about marketing. I was so naïve about that. I thought, 'Write a book. Done.' But you were like, "No, the book is just the beginning." There is this whole machinery behind a book that I never knew existed. I never realised the promotion behind it. I would have been lost without your guidance.

So would you write another book?

Halfway through *Lucky Pennies,* people were already beginning to ask about the next one, saying, "What about book number two?" So that's a really good sign that people were becoming interested in what I had to say. So sitting under a palm tree on a recent holiday, there in the peace and quiet, inspiration floated down on me. I couldn't shake it off. I tried to sunbathe and ignore the feeling, but every time I closed my eyes, I could see the words formulating into sentences in front of me. I rummaged around in my bag and found a pen from the hotel, but I had no paper, so I started writing on the back of my flight confirmation! A few minutes later my next book, *Lucky Pennies: Pennies from Heaven,* was born. I walked barefoot to the little store and bought a notebook and wrote for the rest of the holiday.

I've picked up from where I left off in the original book. I'm a hundred pages in and I'm enjoying it already.

There is still so much to say. My first book came to a natural end when I was looking at another investment property. It was like: this is the house I'm going to buy now; this is why I'm going for this area; this is how I'm going to pay. So in the new book, I will to continue on from here and tell the reader what happened because it did not go quite to plan at all!

There were six potential property sales that went wrong in a year. I would love people to read about that and think, 'My God, she still kept going. She was writing a book and working full-time. But she just wouldn't let go and move on without her third property.' My money pot (the deposit for the house) was getting lower and lower as I was financing my book from it, but then wondrously the right property came along and it was just within my slimmed-down budget.

My message is: don't let problems stop you from going for something. Just do it. You will find a way. Don't think too much. Just make a start and put one foot in front of the other every day, and one day you'll look up and be in a new, wonderful place. Just because the star is in the sky, doesn't mean that you won't grow big enough one day to actually touch it.

IDEAS FOR YOU

- Keep a notebook and jot down notes throughout the day so you don't forget your best ideas.

- Write down tips that you think will help your readers and include these in your book.

- Make the most of train and Tube journeys to get some writing done. Use your coffee breaks and lunch breaks too.

- Use your diary or journal as source material if you feel this will help other people.

- You don't just have to be the "property person" who buys property — include amusing anecdotes too.

- Speak from the heart and be down to earth when you write.

- Consider including sketches, cartoons, or doodles to illustrate your book.

- Aim for seventy thousand words when writing. Decide which subjects you need to expand on and which to leave out.

- Include inspirational quotes that have special meaning for you.

- Get a professional opinion on your manuscript. The bits that you think people won't be interested in may be the bits that are great, and vice versa!

- Writing a book is just the beginning! There must also be promotion to make a book successful.

Acknowledgements

This book would not have been possible without some very special people who I am blessed to have in my life.

Firstly, thank you to all everyone, both friends and clients, who have generously given their time to contribute and share their expertise. Thank you to my incredible team: in particular, Steven Miscandlon for typesetting and Brian Cross for proof-reading.

Thanks to my mum, who conceived me aged 16, but in spite of setbacks and single motherhood went on to become the editor of a regional newspaper. I was fortunate to have a mentor from an early age, when female role models were few and far between.

Thanks to my nan and grandad who took us into their home for many years, and taught us the importance of honesty, integrity, and helping others. They were never afraid to "do different", and encouraged us to do the same.

Thanks to my dad, who raised me from the age of 12, often without the gratitude or recognition he deserved. He's been a rock over the years for all of us.

Thanks to my sister, for sharing the journey, with all its highs and lows.

Thanks to my partner, Chris, for making me laugh at all times of day and night, and being the best person anyone would wish to share their life with.

The biggest thank you goes to my three amazing children, Cormac, Tierni and Chiara, who shine light on the world each and every day. I love you and couldn't have done a page of this without you.

THE AUTHORS' VAULT

FREE Training and Bonuses Specially for You

Topics include:

- How to Find a Publisher or Literary Agent.
- How to Choose a Bestselling Book Title.
- Mistakes to Avoid with Agents and Publishers.
- Red Flags to Look Out For in a Publishing Contract.
- How to Write a Marketing Plan for Your Book.
- Can I Quote Someone Without Permission?
- Should I Use 50 Shades of X as a Book Title?
- How to Write Your Book Faster.
- How to Choose the Best Book Cover.
- Should I Self-Publish or is a Mainstream Publisher Better?
- How to Sell More Copies of your Book.
- How to Stop Other Authors Stealing Your Book Idea.
- Should I Disguise Real-Life Characters?
- How to Get Celebrity Endorsements.
- And much more …

Register for your free reports at:

www.CelebrityAuthorsSecrets.com/vault

OXFORD LITERARY CONSULTANCY
PUBLISHING SERVICES

- **Manuscript evaluation** – confidential feedback of your book's marketability.

- **Proofreading and editing** – with fast-track service.

- **Book cover design and typesetting.**

- **PR campaigns** – publicity in magazines, newspapers, radio and TV.

- **Ghostwriting.**

- **Mentoring.**

Our consultants work for publishers including: Bloomsbury, HarperCollins, Hodder & Stoughton, Little Brown, Simon & Schuster and Random House.

Find out whether your book idea is marketable.
Book a free 20-minute consultation today!

www.oxfordwriters.com

Lightning Source UK Ltd.
Milton Keynes UK
UKOW01f0837180117

292232UK00002B/331/P